CW01486614

The Cult of Saint Catherine of Alexandria in Ireland

By Arthur Spears

Published by Rathmullan and District Local History Society,
Pier House, Rathmullan, Co Donegal, Ireland.
Rathmullan 2006

*Published by Rathmullan District Local History Society,
Pier House, Rathmullan, Co Donegal, Ireland*

*British Library Cataloguing in Publication Data
ISBN: 0-978-0-9540888-1-1*

*Index compilation by P.J. Flanagan, Dunshaughlin, Ireland.
Print origination by I-Design, Donegal Town, Ireland.*

Dedicated to the memory of
Mrs Catherine Emerson *(1922-2004)*
and her husband
Lucius Emerson M.A. *(1911-2005).*
Historians both.

Printed in Ireland by Standard Printers Co. Galway, Ireland.

Saint Catherine of Alexandria by Corravegio
(Courtesy of Lugano Castagnola Gallery, Geneva)
(Currently on view at Museo Thyssen Bornemisza, Madrid)
ISBN: 0-978-0-9540888-1-1

© 2006 Arthur Spears

This publication has been supported by Donegal Local Development Company under the Leader + National Rural Development Programme 2000 - 2006.

Acknowledgments

This survey could not have been put together without the help of many.
It is with great pleasure the author takes this opportunity of thanking them.

M. A. Lyons kindly commented on an early draft but without commenting on the several conjectures put forward. Many of these would certainly exceed what would normally be approved by Dr Lyons for scholarly work. No claim to scholarship, however, is being made by this present writer who has had no academic training in historical studies. Only he alone may be held responsible for any errors of fact or excessive surmise.

Local informants to whom thanks are due are Vincent Garvey of Oristown County Meath. Padraig O Siochrú, Michael O Dubhlanaigh and the late Michaela Connolly of Corca Dhuibhne–Dingle--Denis O'Callaghan and Michael Brown of Killarney—all of County Kerry. Moira Mallon and Hugh O'Donnell of Killybegs, County Donegal, Mr and Mrs William Ward of Fieldstown, Fingal, William Fraher and the late Lawrence Mongey and James O'Keefe ofDungarvan, and Patrick Murphy of Mothel, County Waterford, Charlie Monaghan of Dublin City Council Simon W.Kennedy of New Ross, Co. Wexford; and Christy Roche of Fermoy Co. Cork to all of whom the author is very much obliged for enlightenment on local matters and their ready response to requests for information.

In England, Margaret Whitehead and Barbara Lowe of Keynsham also Noel Murray of Nuneaton helped generously with their time through correspondence

Cathryn Cashman of Conna, and Padraig Mac Amhlaoibh of Cobh, County Cork-, Joanna Carson of Ballymena Co. Antrim, Mary McLaughlin of Aughrim Co. Galway and Donal Smith of Killybegs, Co Donegal all of whom supplied photographs. The artist, Brendan Scally kindly presented his sketch of the ruins of Grace Dieu Nunnery, Lusk, while The Parish of Saint Catherine, Dublin provided the drawing of their church by J.O'Hanlon.

The courtesy of the Public Librarians and their Assistants is acknowledged-in Dublin at NLI, The Catholic Central Library, RIA, RSAI, and An Roinn Bhéaloideas Eireann (U.C.D.); also the Librarians at the County Libraries of Donegal, Cork, Mayo, Waterford and The Western Library Board (NI) V.Rev. Saml. Reede, Dean of Raphoe, Dermot Lynch and Brian O'Neill of Strabane, County Tyrone,. also the late Arthur Lemon of Stradbally, County Waterford provided invaluable ideas, references and literary aid.

Figure No 1 Saint Catherine of Alexandria by Rubens
(Courtesy of The National Gallery of Art, London)

At Lifford, Co. Donegal, Jerh. Drumm prepared the maps and helped at the computer, Ivan Johnston at Donegal Town set up the final editing and P.J. Flanagan prepared the index.Thanks to all of them.

To the several Curators and Cartlannai and their assistants at various locations, the Spanish Embassy, Dublin, 'The Granary' Museum, Waterford, the Dungarvan Town Museum and T.Na G, Co. na Gaillimhe the writer offers thanks for favours granted. Indeed to the many who are inevitably left unmentioned but who contributed in any way, large or small, again many thanks

Thanks are also due, and not the least, to the members of the author's own family, often called upon to sort out the computer but helpful in so many other ways too, with constructive criticism, editing and a great deal of encouragement. The photograph of the **La Girona** artefact is reproduced with the kind permission of the trustees of the National Museums of Northern Ireland. Others are acknowledged within the text. The aerial surveys are courtesy of the Ordnance Survey office and kind permission of the Government of Ireland.

Figure No. 2 Saint Catherine's Holy Well, Killybegs, County Donegal

CONTENTS

Map No.I. IRELAND
Dedications to St. Catherine of Alexandria

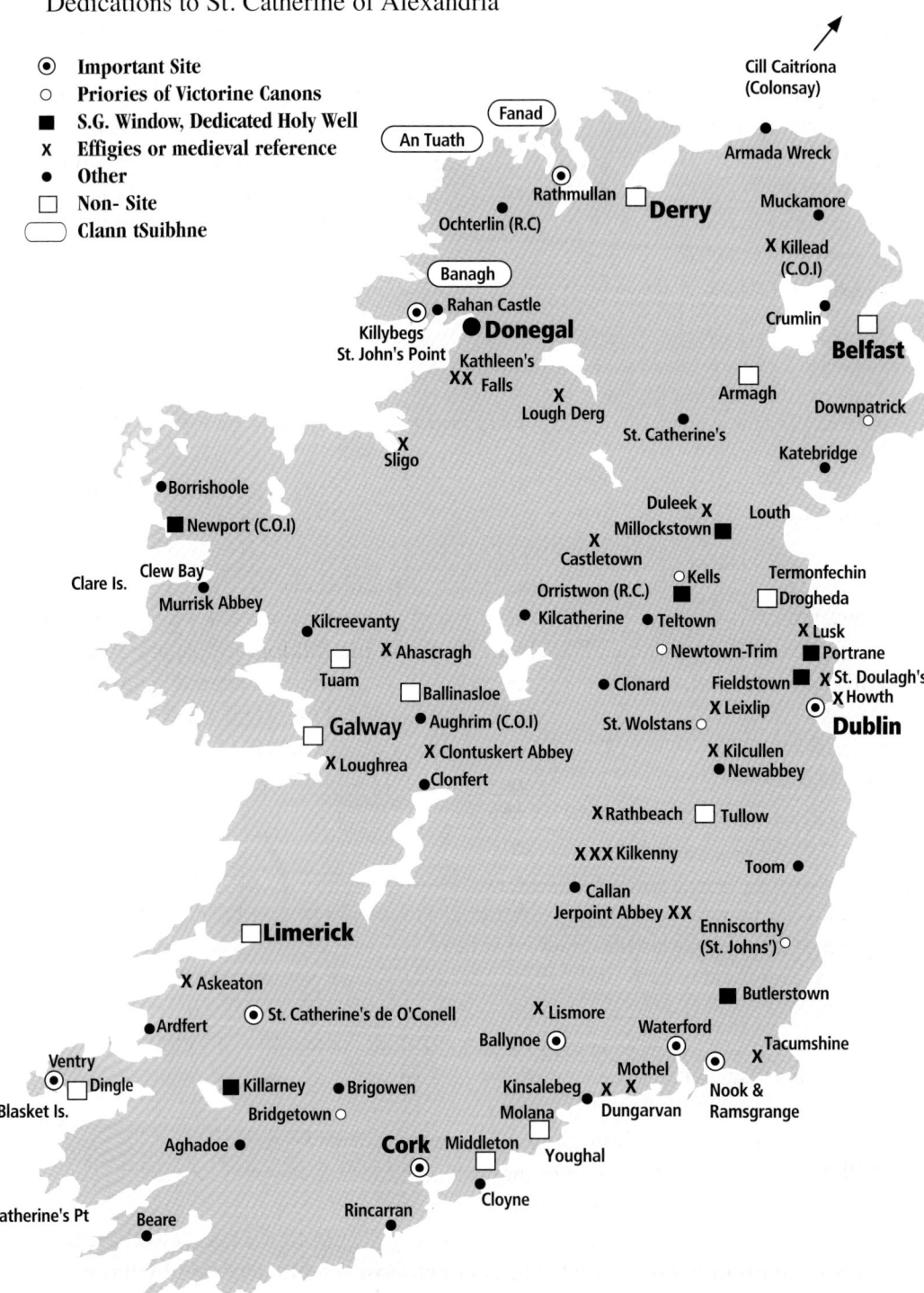

⊙ **Important Site**
○ **Priories of Victorine Canons**
■ **S.G. Window, Dedicated Holy Well**
X **Effigies or medieval reference**
● **Other**
☐ **Non- Site**
⌒ **Clann tSuibhne**

Cill Caitríona
(Colonsay)

Fanad

An Tuath

Armada Wreck

Rathmullan

Derry

Muckamore

Ochterlin (R.C)

X Killead
(C.O.I)

Banagh

Rahan Castle

Crumlin

Killybegs

Donegal

St. John's Point   Kathleen's

XX Falls

Belfast

X
Lough Derg

Armagh

Downpatrick

St. Catherine's

Katebridge

X
Sligo

Borrishoole

Duleek X   Louth

Newport (C.O.I)

Millockstown ■

X
Castletown

Clew Bay

Orristwon (R.C.)   ○ Kells

Termonfechin

Clare Is.

Murrisk Abbey

■ Kilcatherine   ● Teltown

☐Drogheda

Kilcreevanty

○ Newtown-Trim

X Lusk

X Ahascragh

■ Portrane

Tuam

● Clonard

Fieldstown ■ X St. Doulagh's

Ballinasloe

X Leixlip

X Howth

Galway

Aughrim (C.O.I)

St. Wolstans ○

⊙ Dublin

X Loughrea

X Clontuskert Abbey

X Kilcullen

Clonfert

● Newabbey

X Rathbeach ☐ Tullow

X XX Kilkenny

Toom ●

● Callan

Jerpoint Abbey XX

Enniscorthy
(St. Johns') ○

☐Limerick

Butlerstown ■

X Askeaton

X Lismore

● Ardfert

⊙ St. Catherine's de O'Conell

Waterford

Ballynoe ⊙

X Tacumshine

Mothel

Ventry

⊙☐Dingle

■ Killarney ● Brigowen

Kinsalebeg X X

Nook &

Blasket Is.

Bridgetown ○

Molana Dungarvan

Ramsgrange

Aghadoe ●

Cork Middleton ☐

Youghal

Rincarran

Cloyne

St. Catherine's Pt

Beare

Prologue

Should one travel across Ireland from County Kerry to County Donegal in late November one may be surprised, if taking an interest in such matters, to find some penitential practices of the Catholic religion taking place at either end of ones journey and this in honour of the same clearly alien saint. These, as one may ascertain by local enquiry, will be devotions or celebrations for the cult of Saint Catherine of Alexandria, a 'non-Irish saint' whose feast-day is on the twenty fifth of the month. Remarkably, if one similarly takes a zigzag route in between these two counties (see accompanying map p.7) one may come across several such celebrations at other places too - to the same saint and on the same date.

Again referring to the beginning of the aforementioned trip, the customs seen performed at Ventry on the Dingle Peninsula Co. Kerry (for Naomh Caitlín or Caitríona) seem similar to those at the other end of it, that is at Killybegs in County Donegal, (for Saint Catharine). Other sites where the saint is patronised (to be mentioned below) will also be found much alike in their traditions.

There can be no doubt that it is the one saint (of the several Catherines) who is honoured in the various parts of the country, as the feast day on which the rites are performed is the same. The origin stories in the folklore for Ventry and Killybegs are somewhat similar. At Ventry the folklore mentions a shipwreck, a lone survivor coming ashore but shortly dying and being interred at a venerable burial ground. There is now a church there dedicated to Naomh (Saint) Caitriona. Also at Killybegs, a stricken ship comes into harbour after a stormy passage and a bishop (a passenger of the ship) blesses a Holy Well as a memorial of the ship's safe arrival, dedicating it to Saint Catherine. Saint Catherine's name is preserved in these two forms in the folklore and ordinary speech of each district. While at Ventry the traditions surrounding the saint give Rome as her place of origin; at Killybegs there is closer agreement with the 'official' Life of the saint. There was a fortuitous introduction of a competent version of the Life into the locality in the sixteenth century. In manuscript form it claimed Alexandria in Egypt to be Saint Catherine's place of origin as standard.

Three accounts explain how Saint Catherine came to be associated with the Killybegs site. Each has its own interest. The basic facts have long been available for the version which will be advanced in these pages by an unfortunate reference in the Annals of the Four Masters, which hid the background, clear facts have become discredited. The account most readily accepted by those frequenting the Holy Well at Killybegs, today is that the cult of Saint Catherine is Coptic in origin, and came directly from Egypt or through the aforementioned bishop who blessed the Holy Well.

In the form propagated by **Canon Maguire** in his *History of the Diocese of Raphoe* supplied[1] what appears to be a close approximation to the truth, (that is that knowledge of Saint Catherine came with the Anglo Normans in the twelfth century) and devotees are normally satisfied with this. The following dissertation will attempt to delve more deeply into the facts available and by looking at the several places where the Life of Saint Catherine is celebrated to examine the history of the saints cults and get closer to the remarkable attraction the saint has had for so many people of every kind for over one and a half millennia.

As already stated, Saint Catherine of Alexandria is known, besides at Ventry or Killybegs, in a number of other places in Ireland. In these places, while her name and sanctity may not be equally well remembered, the sites known to the author call for a little discussion. Very few of them are now attended annually by devotees but there is in most cases some memory of people attending in times gone by at a 'Pattern' on the Saint's Day. Many such Patterns are almost wholly forgotten; whatever slight recollection there may be often arises through the modicum of historical interest aroused, by the saint's unusual 'non-Irish' name, as written into local accounts.....

The opportunity is taken here to remark that at Ramsgrange, in County Wexford, Saint Catherine and Saint James are joint patrons of the parish. Both of these saints are also curiously associated, at Dublin by the parishes of Saint Catherine and Saint James in the Dublin Liberties which adjoin. The Church (C.O.I) at Donore Avenue, in the parish of Saint Catherine, was originally called 'St. Victor's' but is now dedicated to Saint Catherine and Saint James. The parish was probably part of a joint parish under the name of both saints originally. The chapel which used to exist in the nearby former St. Thomas' Court, Dublin was dedicated to Saint James and Saint Catherine. (according to **Myles Ronan** in *Archivium Hibernicum VIII* (1941). Although, as may be seen from the (1634) Plan at page 11 herein, it only shows a "Saint Catherine" church.) Also at Dingle, Co. Kerry one part of the parish is dedicated to St. James, while the other, (Ventry, Ceann Trá) has Naomh Caitríona supreme. (The extent of the walls of Dingle seems to have encompassed that portion of the parish called for St James and, according to **Saml. Lewis's** *Dictionary (1837)*- it was first colonised by Spaniards the adoption of the saint in the "town" part may be partly accounted for)

---

[1] See Appendix 1

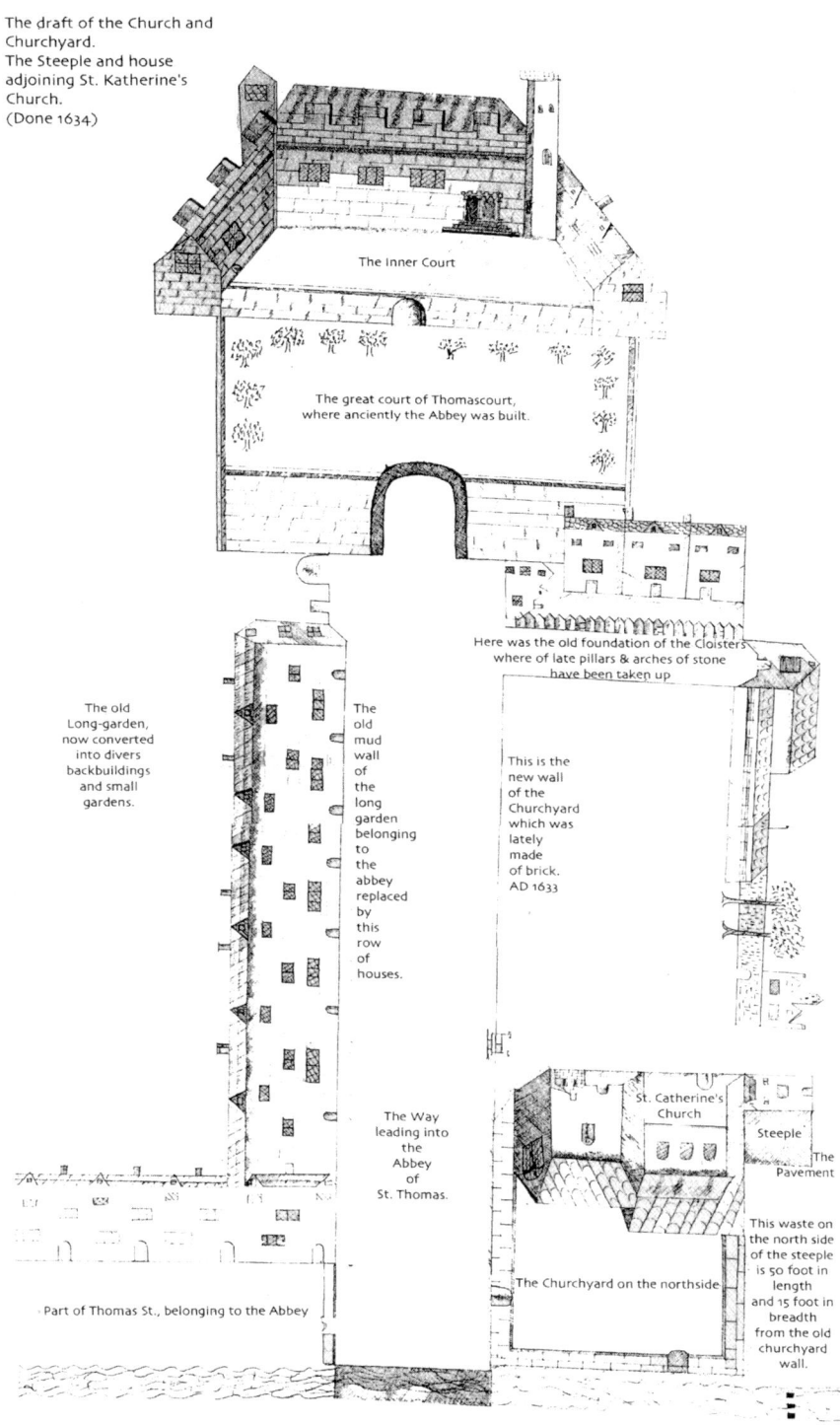

The draft of the Church and Churchyard.
The Steeple and house adjoining St. Katherine's Church.
(Done 1634)

The Inner Court

The great court of Thomascourt, where anciently the Abbey was built.

Here was the old foundation of the Cloisters where of late pillars & arches of stone have been taken up

The old Long-garden, now converted into divers backbuildings and small gardens.

The old mud wall of the long garden belonging to the abbey replaced by this row of houses.

This is the new wall of the Churchyard which was lately made of brick. AD 1633

The Way leading into the Abbey of St. Thomas.

St. Catherine's Church

Steeple

The Pavement

This waste on the north side of the steeple is 50 foot in length and 15 foot in breadth from the old churchyard wall.

The Churchyard on the northside

Part of Thomas St., belonging to the Abbey

Thomas Street.

St. James Street

Plan (1634) of the Abbey of Saint Thomas the Martyr in the Liberties of Dublin, (Courtesy of National Library of Ireland)

The reason for this association of saints is not fully understood; a rather speculative explanation is given at page 39 below. St James Major was popular amongst the Anglo-Normans also; (Feast Day 25th July) An early grantee of land in the Liberties of Dublin bearing the name 'Palmer' had presumably completed the pilgrimage to Compostella and the tomb of San Iacobo.

Some References Consulted

A useful source of information used in preparing this survey/article has been Katherine J. Lewis's *The Cult of St Katherine of Alexandria in Late Medieval England* [2]. This work- focuses on the spread of the cult throughout England and how it was taken up especially after the arrival there of the Norman king, William the First, 'The Conqueror'. Cult sites and bequests under wills etc. are given in her book which are of interest for Ireland. The methodology employed by this author also provides a lead on to how to proceed with a similar exploration /study for Ireland.

While examining the matter it was noted by this present writer that the name of Saint Mary's Abbey, Keynsham in Somerset, England kept coming through as having lands in Ireland. It also appeared that its canons (members of the Order) may have had a missionary involvement with presenting the cult of Saint Catherine. Canons from Keynsham were supplied to Irish Abbeys dedicated to Saint Catherine. The making of these dedications may however have been more influenced by the king, his mother and his brother John. The Royals were endeavouring to encourage the success of these abbeys and it may have been this rather than any desire of the canons to propagate the cult that was the source of the dedications.

The Royals had evidently became attracted to the devotion of Saint Catherine during their stay at Anjou and then at Bristol. The cult was strong among the Rouennaise (especially those having Norse antecedents). One of Henry's earliest objectives as Duke of Anjou was the annexing of Rouen to his Normandy dukedom. A consequence of this was an increase in his appreciation of the Gallo-Norse element of the population, which was strong at the time there[3] and also in that part of Ireland he was intent in taking for himself which was Dublin and along the south coast.

---

[2] Woodbridge 2000 (Henchforth referred to as **Lewis** 2000)

[3] A similar Norse ethos was an ingredient in the make-up of the population of areas of Ireland with which Kings Henry II and John found themselves closely associated. In their short reigns it may be noted they concentrated much of their activities amongst them. This presumption is quite consistent with a rapid spread of the cult of Saint Catherine. **Douglas Jarrold** in his *History of England* (London 1949) p.496, notes Henry "had little religion and no morals" but this was in later life when matters of state took up most of his attention. As a young man and still under the influence of his mother this may not have been so.

The useful *Women and the Church in Medieval Ireland* (1140 to 1540) by **Dianne Hall**[4] was received too late to incorporate more than a few of the author's ideas. It contains a copious bibliography of the Irish church in the medieval period. Other books utilised are listed below in A Selection of Book References Consulted (page 109)

Figure No 3 Photograph of sculpture of Saint Catherine from the ruined convent of Black Nuns near Foynes Co. Limerick. (It lies beside the former fortress, Shanid, of the Earls of Desmond (ca. 1300-1600) (From, **Hall** 2003)

---

[4]N.B The Monastieum Hibernium project at NUI Maynooth mainly concerns the 13th Century and earlier but will, it seems certain, prove invaluable as a source for scholars of the period. Saint Catherine does not feature in DrAilbhe Mac Samhrain's account in *Medievel Dublin*. Perhaps his project may examine the probability of substitutions of her name for early Saints or holy wells.

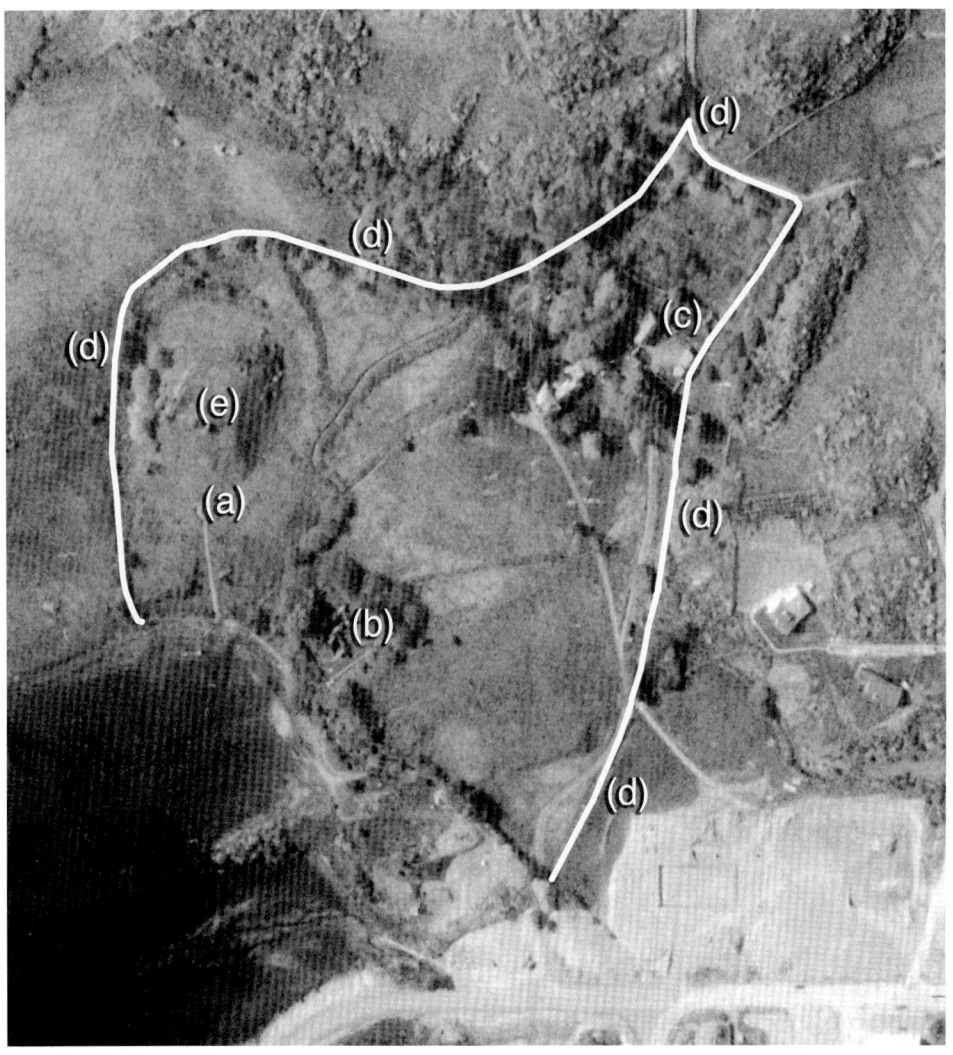

Map No. II Aerial Survey of Killybegs showing:
(a) Holy Well (Saint Catherine's)
(b) Old Friary Cealla Beaga Site and Plantation Church
(c) C. of 1. Rectory ("Saint Catherine's")
(d) Boundary of pre Commonwealth Church Lands
(e) Kit's "Castle" (an Admiralty gun emplacement)

CHAPTER 1

The origin of The Irish cult of Saint Catherine of Alexandria - an overview.

The Christian Roman Emperors, took up the cult with enthusiasm practically from its inception in Egypt. It swept through to the western seaboard where it halted in the eleventh century as if awaiting some new surge of energy. Later it will be seen how this was kindled but attention must first be turned to Ireland towards the end the twelfth century where it was already beginning to show a presence.

Two strands of evolution of the cult of Saint Catherine in Ireland, will be concentrated on. The first coincided with the initial colonisation of the southern half of the country by the Anglo-Normans. This ethnically diverse group had been forging an alliance between armed adventurers in Wales and the South West of England—Herefordshire, Gloucestershire and Somerset— from early in the twelfth century, and were looking for something to do when Diarmaid Mac Murchú sought out Duke Henry The history of the late twelfth century invasion of Ireland thereafter is well known and need not be repeated at length.

The principal points of entry of the Anglo-Normans were through Dublin and its immediate hinterland, the so-called 'Pale' (that is the area they were soon to refer to as that 'where the common law runs'). The proto-cities of Waterford, Cork and Limerick also became hubs centred on potentially rich countryside soon to be settled by them. They were followed shortly by new waves of settlers intent on entering upon the remaining apparently 'free land'. It was but sparsely inhabited. Radiating rapidly from the aforementioned entry points and other landing places their numbers increased so as to form further small Anglo-Norman Pales coalescing into a single Anglo-Norman Munster by the fourteenth century. Included among the incomers were monks, canons, priests and bishops. It is thought the Saint Catherine's cult came about the same time, perhaps presented mainly by missionary clergy from the Bristol Channel (an idea to be expanded upon later). It was happily accepted principally by an indigenous population of Hiberno-Norse or Ostmen who had occupied the coastlands and for whom there is some suggestion of an early familiarity with the Saint. (These people of Viking antecedents had for centuries been settling in the coastal areas among the friendly Irish while continuing to trade with Cambro Norse along the Bristol-Channel, and the Gallo-Norse of Normandy and Aquitaine even the Spanish. If they had been already acquainted with Saint Catherine it was to the great satisfaction of the clerics among the new Anglo-Norman arrivals not to say the new King Henry II, a presumed devotee himself.[5]

Another strand, that associated with County Donegal in the North of the country,took place somewhat later and was of Connacht origin. It was not entirely without its roots or independent of the former. The Anglo-Normans (by now 'English') had come in strength to Connacht under the Tudor Lords in the fifteenth century their predecessors brought missions from the Pales to a province already partially assimilated to English ways. Importantly nuns or canonesses following the Augustinian rule served much of the new ethos.

One native Irishwoman from Connacht, Máire MacSuibhne,[6] a Tir Conaill (County Donegal) Chief's wife, took up the cult of Saint Catherine, petitioning the saint, this present writer believes, because of the prevalence amongst her husbands clan of the sin of kin-slaying. She herself was a native of County Mayo, in Connacht, and is thought to have received the devotion to the saint within her own rather religious family. The Tir Conaill Clan to which she had tied herself was notoriously given to internal conflict over the succession to the chieftainships. There is reason to believe that during her lifetime as chief's wife she endeavoured to reduce these revenge killings between family members by introducing better religion into her husband's territory—notoriously unsuccessfully in the matter of her own son as it turned out.

The dissemination of the cult and its retreat

While the Anglo-Normans in their early areas of settlement of the land were at least among the earliest to introduce Saint Catherine to Ireland, her cult extended by a process of gradual assimilation under several name-forms (Santa Catharina /Catalina Caitriona, Katherine /Catherine, Ina, —Naomh /San/ Cataríona/Caitríona Caitlín / Cáit (often pronounced 'Kit'), Saint Kathleen, and Kate). The saint was eventually treated widely as if fully Irish. In the period following the first phase of the Anglo-Norman colonisation of the Meath Pale proper, (followed by the Leinster and Munster Pales), the cult of Saint Catherine in Ireland was confined at first

---

[5] See footnotes No 3 & 24
[6] See footnote No 110

---

among the settlers themselves but was eventually taken up by native clerics. The colony expanded still further. Historical and archaeological researchers have shown the process of Romanisation of the Celtic Church. It did not initially penetrate into Connacht and the North West. Yet the settlers kept coming in great numbers, going into remote parts, or wherever they wished to plant their farms with some security. By the end of the fourteenth century new arrivals were bringing with them priests, patron saints and other cultural baggage along with their families. Even though some of them were to later adopt the Irish language and other customs yet they never thought of themselves as other than English.

The Dublin area was initially the focus of the first arrivals from 1170, the influx to Meath/Kildare area and Waterford, Cork and Limerick, following soon after. The Ulster Earldom was left largely to its own devices, originating in a desire of the King to provide a balance and to prevent the Leinster/Munster magnates from becoming too strong. In Ulster, besides, the invasion was more resolutely resisted over a longer period by the native septs than occurred in the midlands and farther south. Even in the midlands there was sporadic resistance. There was a serious uprising sponsored by the Scottish King Bruce and his brother in 1300. However the Scots in combination with the Irish were successfully held off from Louth and Dublin in 1317.

When the news of the Pale being surrounded was heard in England, the 'New English' became somewhat discouraged. Settler families came in smaller numbers than before and most of the midland areas went into a period of temporary decline in colonisation. The Munster lords mainly Butler and Desmonds, however, persisted in establishing their power bases. They were well supported by churchmen from England during the fourteenth and fifteenth centuries. A resurgence followed, especially during the period, from the reign of Henry VIII to the end of the reign of James 1st. More settlers then ever came and the Reformation began to take full effect.

With the onset of the powerful plantations of Ireland and the monastic suppressions which followed, there began a decline of individual saints' cult, but also of other practices of the old religion. After the Henrician Dissolution of the monasteries there was little support for any saint's cult in any part of the country, even amongst the fugitive Roman clergy after 1550.

The Dissolution took a little longer in West Munster and Connacht, because of rebellions there, during which even the most zealous of Elizabethan commanders were unable to go in. Saint Catherine's cult seems however to have lasted sporadicacally in these areas (until, it is suspected—, perhaps only because of the absence of surviving records to it— it seems almost to have petered out in the modern period after 1600). Except in a certain few parishes, about which accounts will be given below, local devotions continued to be held at Holy Wells where Saint Catherine 'patterns'/'rounds' (penitential rites) had been performed. Even at these places where her name still survives, traditional knowledge of the saint is today low; a mention of Saint Catherine's name rarely giving rise to more than mild questionings about her. A further aim of this essay is, if possible, to provide some answers about a much neglected saint and perhaps to help to redress this state of affairs a little.

Inevitably the lack of documentary evidence has hampered research into the saint and how her Irish cult developed or declined. In the places associated with her name, from a simple Holy Well dedication, right up to small ruins complete with effigeal representations, or even an old abbey called after her, it is rare that primary documentation survives. It is sometimes that only through association of the saint with an abbey in England which had properties in Ireland that some corroborative information may fortuitously turn up in its English archives. For this present exploration some sites to be mentioned later require a little conjecture, building from pitifully small pieces of information often surviving in a weak tradition only. While such may often raise more questions than are easily answered they sometimes provide clues for where to begin.

The word 'cult' is used in this article in preference to 'cultus' for the rituals surrounding saintly worship even though it has more recently been informally appropriated for use exclusively by esoteric groups for their devotions.

Figure No. 4 Detail from "The Last Judgement" from a fresco by **Michelangelo** in The Sistine Chapel at the Vatican, showing Saint Catherine displaying the instruments of her martyrdom.

CHAPTER 2

Some Further Perspectives of this Presentation

The following exposition tries to detail how the cult of Saint Catherine of Alexandria was introduced from England in the twelfth century and still survives in a few places in Ireland. It examines a little of the history of the cult and its relevance to sites where the saint's name is still remembered or recorded, though the devotion itself may have long since lapsed.

At first, in order to be popular in Ireland non-Irish saints required to have had some reference being made to them by the compilers of early Calendars listing saints approved at Rome. Those saints were of particular interest to those who drew up *The Martyrology of Oengus* [7], and *The Martyrology of Tallaght* [8] (ninth century) and *The Calendar of Gorman* (twelfth century). The Irish saints were honoured in their various traditional birthplaces, at their monastic sites and at various places within their 'paruchia' where their cult was practised. Genealogies, the preparation of which the scribes were adept, listed many of the saints' family relationships. Many of the saints listed in *M.Tallaght* received recognition through their traditional association with a particular district, though occasionally with an Anglo-Saxon saint mentioned by the Venerable Bede[9] in his works as having visited Ireland. The works of Saint Jerome were scoured for suitable continental saints. Saint Catherine though from the Mid-East, when introduced to Ireland was nevertheless rather surprisingly, quickly adopted by the native Irish from the thirteenth century on. She is first mentioned in an Irish language context in the twelfth century *Calendar of Gorman* though some believe her efficacy as patron was popular amongst the female religious somewhat earlier than this. The same saint continued, of course, to be the client of the many incoming colonials, (soldiers, farming settlers, and churchmen for whom she had been a familiar figure in the spirituality of the old country).

---

[7] **Whitley Stokes** (Ed.) *The Martyrology of Oengus the Culdee* (London 1905)
[8] **R.J. Best** and **H.J. Lawlor** (Eds) *The Martyrology of Tallaght* (London 1931)
[9] See **Padraig O Riain** *The Tallaght Martyrologies Redated* in Cambridge Medieval Celtic Studies (Winter 1990) also his *Anglo-Saxon Ireland The evidence of The Martyrology of.Tallaght* (Cambridge (1993). Saint Catherine's name fails to appear in the compilation of references to nearly 5000 saints from pre Anglo Norman times in *Corpus Genealgiarum Sanctorum Hibernia (Dublin 1985)* prepared by the same author.

This present survey ranges over Irish literature, history and hagiography and was aided by material derived from visits to sites where Saint Catherine was honoured. Upon these visits much information was obtained from helpful local informants.

Following the coming of The Anglo-Normans the cult spread among the native population from several centres throughout the early-colonised areas. It seems to have been well known already amongst the Hiberno-Norse. It was generally discouraged along with the monasteries in the sixteenth century but did not die out altogether. Theories will be developed here presently of how it remains still active at Ventry, Co Kerry, Ballynoe, Co Cork Lough Derg and Killybegs in County Donegal also Oristown, Co Meath. For the Dublin area, Thomas Street/ Meath Street etc-St Catherine's Parish -and Counties Kildare and Meath, ecclesiastical historians of the medieval period have provided much data[10]. For sites in Counties Cork, Limerick, Galway, Mayo, and Waterford a little survives. Special attention will be given to the parishes of Ramsgrange, County Wexford, Killead and Muckamore at Co.Antrim and Abbeyside County Waterford where, because of lack of local information, certain inferences will have to be drawn from such slight evidence as comes to hand. The reader will be asked to accept that this is necessary for completeness sake. The mythology of the Teltown area of County Meath is searched for an explanation for the Saint Catherine cult's survival there, which it appears to have done against all odds.

---

[10] The papers of **V.Rev. M.V.Ronan** in *Archiviiun Hibernicum* Vol VIII (Maynooth 1941*) The Royal Visitation of Dublin 1615* and *Archbishop Bulkeley's Visitation of Dublin 1630* are very useful for Dublin churche. Also in the same series Vol IV, **Rev.M. A. Murphy** does similar service for the former diocese of Ardfert. (The name is still included in that of the United C.O.I Diocese of Limerick, Aghadoe and Ardfert) These articles will be referred to as 'R(1615) or RV(1630)'

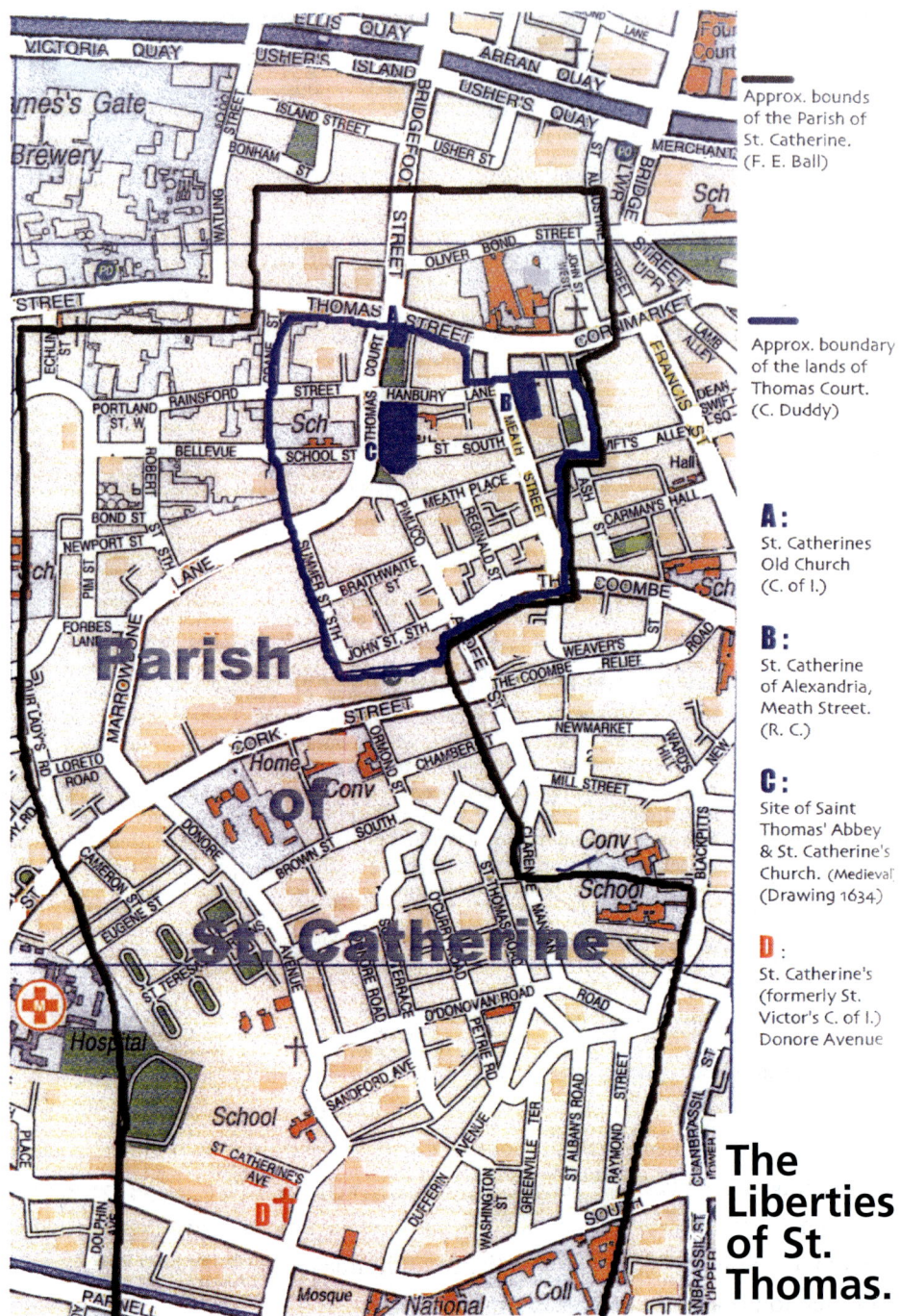

MAP No. III Map of the Dublin Liberties showing The Parish of Saint Catherine (As extracted from
F.Elrington Ball's *History of the County of Dublin Part IV* (1906) and entered on the 4 miles to one inch inch
Map of the City of Dublin by Permission of the Government (Ordnance Survey of Ireland).Permit
No.MP006804. See also maps provided by **Andrew Halpin** with his paper *Development Phases in Hiberno
Norse*, Dublin: "A tale of two cities" in **Sean Duffy's** (Ed) *Medieval Dublin VI* (Dublin 2005)

How in general the Cult of the Saints Developed

This survey is not meant to be a Life of Saint Catherine, but rather a description of how her cult began in the Middle East in the fifth century and progressed from there. There were indeed several Lives of Saint Catherine, some purporting to begin from early in the Christian era. From these early times mention is often made in saints Lives of miraculous occurrences. These were introduced in conjunction with established facts of contemporary 'profane' history by way of verisimilitude! The miraculous, if relating to the society and the customs of the author's time, received more attention than they would otherwise get from those serious early historians. Some modem scholars of history have indeed delved into these Lives receiving insights acceptable as respectable history. They have extracted useful information which the ancient authors unwittingly provided. (from Sometimes unique references to material otherwise unavailable to historians).It is the present writer's wish particularly to trace the cult of Saint Catherine of Alexandria from its arrival on Irish shores and if thereby, to suggest some consequences which might be taken up by the scholarly. It is also hoped that these suggestions will complement and encourage work of a similar kind coming from those interested both inside and outside academia.

In general, 'early saints' Lives were not always intended to provide just a series of factual data relating to the saint being treated but rather to present accounts framed for the edification of the reader. The Lives of Saint Catherine, clearly of Eastern Europe or Mid-East origin, were, often, of this type. In the making of ordinary early saints lives, special attention was given to those few who, because of heroic lives, or who had suffered martyrdom like the apostles, were judged worthy of entrance into the kingdom of heaven. They were accorded the title of 'Saint' and detailed Lives were written of them so that their virtues should become widely known. Following these writings public veneration was the next step in establishing the saint's 'cult' guaranteeing his or her holiness by noting miraculous cures taking place after their death. The special benefits which might be received following intercession by clients of the saint were pointed out. These could be invoked by prayer, works of asceticism, pilgrimage, or donations to a shrine dedicated to the saint.

Recognition of sainthood was mainly undertaken through the establishment of a feast marking the date of the saints "nativity", that of his or her reception by God into new life in the heavenly kingdom - the date of his or her death. A 'translation' of the remains of the saint to a new church in the persons honour was important. Along with this came veneration of the saint's relics. On the continent this seems to have taken off following the reception by the bishop of Rouen, Veritricius, of the relics of Roman martyrs which he enshrined in his church a little before AD 400. The practice blossomed widely from then on.[11]

Ireland was slow in the use of relics for developing the cult of saints. Objects such as the crosiers (in reality often just their walking sticks), gospel books or bells which the missionaries had brought with them were preserved and became venerated as memorials. They were often enshrined in beautiful reliquary boxes. Little was known at first about these 'Celtic' saints on the continental mainland. Neither did the continental idea and practice of honouring saints bones penetrate Ireland for their special powers for a long time. In due course, however, Irish churchmen made their way to Italy for actual personal relics for the liturgical rites which required them. This seems to have arisen from the veneration of bones from the Catacombs from which there appeared to be no shortage of supply. Before that the type of 'relic' which was initially brought back to Ireland from the continent may have been just a piece of the saint's clothing or something that had merely touched the saint's body.[12] The veneration of the native saints at home was generally supported by knowledge of their original place of foundation of their mission, their burial sites within their enclosure (caiseal or lios) being pointed out (along with the wells from which their monks drew water). Later still, the church site (ceall, Latin 'cella') central to the saint's 'paruchia' (or 'family') or other place claimed visited by them was honoured by his or her name being attached to it. Some seventh to tenth century accounts exist of important founder saint's actual bones being carried throughout his Irish paruchia long after his death—not necessarily for cultic purposes but often for promulgating a tax upon outlying churches disclaiming that the saint had ever been there during his lifetime. It is not certain that the bones themselves were promoted as having in themselves any curative or spiritual efficacy. This was to come later resulting in the complete disappearance of such relics of the Celtic saints in Ireland over the centuries.

---

[11] This present writing owes much to the 'Introduction' to **Thomas Head's** *Medieval Hagiography* (London 2001). **Kenneth Woodward's** *Making Saints –How the Catholic Church determines who becomes a Saint* (New York 1996) was also seen.
[12] See **E.O Carragain's** *Bede and The city of Rome* (Jarrow Lecture 1994) p.5, and note 16 p. 49

In the eleventh century a talent for creating artistic reliquaries for gospel books was recognised among settled Norsemen (No doubt their art was imported from Scandinavia) The suggestion was then made that perhaps they should turn to making worthy receptacles for their books or perhaps body-parts of the deceased holy persons. Some fine artefacts soon appeared such as The Shrine of Saint Lachtin's Arm. This was a twelfth century reliquary[13] made to contain the saint's radius, ulna and hand bones. (The contents were lost over the centuries, the fate of practically all relics of the early Irish saints.)

About this time (eleventh century) on the continent, the matter of the authenticity of relics began to exercise the minds, of the papacy. Also the genuineness of the holy persons put forward for sainthood was beginning to be questioned. Some writers who prepared accounts of the lives of newly discovered saints had, after their own death, themselves begun to receive a precarious sainthood. Cults sprang up about them, in some cases supplanting traditional saints of considerable vintage. Also the bringing of donations by 'clients' to pilgrimage sites (in anticipation of success of their petitions following the hardship of travel while on the pilgrimage and of the subsequent devotions) was noticed to be open to abuse in the matter of sharp practice. This was particularly the case in Europe where many shrines and their associated churches were being enlarged using the gifts received.

Again, word sometimes got put around that some relics had been stolen by competing shrines, that doubtful relics were being presented for veneration or even that uncertainty was being deliberately raised in regard to the authenticity of relics through doubts being manufactured by jealous competitors. It became clear that a central authority was needed for authentication purposes. Some saints whose historicities were considered doubtful, were suddenly refused the rites of an official cult of the Universal Church, and a long period intervened while the central authority made up their minds. As late as 1969 (as discussed in note below) a large number of popular saints were excluded from the Roman Catholic Calendar for the lack of a proper history. None of the traditional Irish saints, even Saint Patrick, Saint Columba or Saint Brighid, the National Patrons, fail to appear on The Official Calendar. They were allowed in, however, to a secondary list which permitted a Solemnity on their Feast Day. The Pope and the Holy Office were, of course,

---

[13] See **G.F. Mitchell, P.Harbison, L. & M. de Paor and R.A. Stally** (Eds.)
Treasures of Irish Art, 1500 B.C.-1500 A.D (.New York 1977)

concerned at the possibility of actual fraud being perpetrated, and they introduced the rite of Canonisation requiring legalistic Inquiries into the lives of reputed saints and the authenticity of their relics. (The process itself was called 'canonisation') Some important National Saints patronised by the faithful, even those who would be of doubtful authenticity today, were allowed.

Holy persons would not be permitted entry to the primary lists or to be called 'Saints", nor be provided with an official cult, unless they were apostolic. or been declared to have received the honour through canonisation. The only Celtic saint receiving this distinction was Saint Dewi (or David, Feast first March, Patron of Wales), who was canonised in 1120 by Pope Calixtus II.[14] Neither have many of the female Mid- East saints been canonised, Saint Margaret of Antioch, Saint Mary of Egypt, Saint Catherine of Alexandria......

The cult of one's favourite saint was in previous times transmitted often by someone inspired with the mission of doing so, initially by devout monks or other clerical persons. Later, outside of Ireland and Britain, even not having some local attribution, a church dedication, or a Holy Well with a good repute for curative miracles associated with it., cults could easily die out; that is unless accompanied by canonisation papers. Holy Wells especially were prone to loss of their original saint's dedication perhaps only to be resurrected much later by the people of the locality. Otherwise not having been strong in the traditions of the locality, they could be replaced by some different new saint or person of holy repute. It has been noted in such latter cases that the name of the new saint will almost invariably be similar in verbal sound to the one lost. This spontaneous 're-sanctification', will normally be of an 'authentic' national or canonised saint. (Later will be mentioned how this was to occur in at least one important case for Saint Catherine in Ireland.)

It is indeed true that having no canonised saints themselves, the Holy Wells of the Irish were wide open to having authoritative visitors introduce their own personal patrons as a replacement for the defunct entity. If the name of the previous was pagan in appearance or not well remembered, not having a credible 'provenance' not to say canonisation all would be well. In such circumstances a

---

[14] **Canon O'Hanlon's** *Lives of the Irish Saints* Vol III p. 42

cleric proclaiming his own favourite saint for acceptance of his cult would have an easy substitution. The presence of a cleric promoting a change need not always be the active agency. The memory of even a previously strongly held patron saint may die out due to the migration of families away from the locality or, (a not infrequent occurrence for those times) a massacre or plague wiping out a whole district. A completely different saint brought in by those resettling would simply replace the forgotten old with a new, an abandoned church or a considerable spring/well receiving a new dedication.

The Sainthood of Catherine of Alexandria

For Ireland, that the cult of Saint Catherine of Alexandria came with the Anglo-Normans is generally accepted. The evidence for the Ostmen possibly having a part in it is not easy to pin down but sufficient examples will appear below for it to be comfortably tolerated. (That it came from Britain with particular strength at the end of the twelfth century is an acceptable conclusion though clear contacts between ethnic Norse- related groups from France and Ireland in early 12th century evidently playing a part. Several Holy Wells and church sites attest to the presence of Saint Catherine's cult in the Dublin - Louth-Kildare area, which strong in Anglo-Norman presence was intermixed with a leaven of Hiberno-Norse. The Anglo-Normans arriving as Cork felt obliged to drive out the Ostmen; at Waterford they came to some accommodation with them.

To the district of Killybegs, County Donegal, an important cult-site, it arrived later. The survival of the cult there is accounted for by a reference in the Annals to Saint Catherine's efficacy in protecting the town from attack in 1513: also the presence of a Holy Well dedicated in her name (which appears to be a traditional penitential site of some antiquity having an alike sounding name - see below) reinforces the issue. The local tradition at Killybegs that Saint Catherine's cult was brought there by early Coptic monks is still paramount. It is hoped that this present dissertation may dispel such an idea.[15] **Moira Mallon's** article in *Dearcu* (1995), the Ardara Historical Society's annual magazine, makes the best possible plea for it.[16]

---

[15] **H.C. Lawlor** propounded the theory of hermits wishing to get away to the most remote solitude possible and proceeding to Sceilig Mhicil oft the Kerry coast. (Continued over)

Figure No. 5 Ancient Gateway (built up). Supposedly a remnant of the Priory of Saint Catherine, Leixlip (13th century).

[15] (Continued)This he did in an article for the publication *The Church of Ireland A. D. 432 – 1932* (Dublin 1932) prepared for the centenary of Saint Patrick's arrival to Ireland 'proclaiming Pachomian monasticism'. He pointed to its similarities with Coptic monasticism. The appearance of Coptic Cross-types and flabella on grave slabs found on west coast of Ireland pilgrimage sites is truly remarkable, and calls for explanation from archaeologists. (See **Michael Herity's** 'Map of the Chi-ro crosses in Ireland' in *Picard* (1995) p.232. **Joseph Rafferty** in his Paper *Ex Oriente* (JRSAI 1965) has urged caution. That advice applies to any suggestion that the cult of Saint Catherine might have come with them. Moira Mallon refers to a collection of extracts from Mid-Eastern documents made by Prof F.C. Amato of New York about "The Seven Monks of Egypt" providing evidence for a literacy trail to the West.
[16] See the article by **Justine McCarthy** *The Coptic Connection* in *Irish Independent Supplement 'Egypt'* (5th October 2000)

CHAPTER 3

Introduction

The earliest full written Life of Saint Catherine which survives is by one Simon Metaphrastes and comes from the eight century. It is written in Greek. Catherine seems to have been little known even in Egypt at that time though her relics were deposited at an early monastic site at Mount Sinai, through the interest of the Emperor Constantine (311-337). Moreover in the early part of the sixth century, the Emperor Justinian (527-565) formally founded the great Holy Monastery of Mount Sinai, Saint Catherine's resting-place. Her relics being reported to have curative properties, together, of course, with the reputed saintliness of the monks themselves, may have prompted the latter Emperor's action. (Alternatively he may simply have wished to honour the nearby Mountain of Moses). Thereafter, however knowledge of the saint spread by several vernacular lives through many parts of Eastern Europe before the eleventh century. These Lives received several embellishments as they were transmitted. Returning crusaders to France brought a fully developed *Life* back with them. It was brought thence to England and her cult progressed there, eventually arriving at Ireland.

This apparently rather late presence of the cult in Ireland is essentially due to its popularity among Anglo-Norman clerics and their followers coming in at the end of the twelfth century. King Henry II died in 1189 but obviously his foundation strategy for the Invasion of Ireland was extremely well laid, even down to matters appertaining to religion. One must admire his ability as an administrator.

Afterwards new priories and churches came but depended largely upon the predilection of the new magnates for their foundations. These men felt independent and did not ask to be informed of administrative considerations. A previous knowledge of the saint among the population of Ostmen was an advantage.and aided the cult's acceptance. The evident coincidence of the cult's earliest distribution (to be indicated below) and the location of the places where the Ostmen had settled seems significant. A number of religious houses were also founded in the thirteenth century straight away (some not in Hiberno-Norse areas) by founders one would have expected to promote Saint Catherine but did not do so. Explanations will be sought. Those involved were prominent Anglo Norman settlers whose retinue of ecclesiastics[17] -clearly at the instance of King John- were. "to be nourished as useful agents in the affairs of State", as phrased by **Revd. Elliott**.

Except for the apparent Ostman connection, no special pattern can be discerned in the distribution of the new religious houses dedicated to Saint Catherine. Dedications to her churches, priories, abbeys are notably absent outside of places not heavily settled by the Hiberno-Norse. The placing of three large Abbeys to her name in dioceses whose bishops had been consecrated at Canterbury, i.e. at Cork. Dublin and Waterford, seems to have resulted mainly from deliberate policy. At the beginning, these abbeys were supplied with canons from Somerset: especially noticeable being the number coming from the order of Canons Regular of Saint Augustine of the community of Saint Victor. This particular Order was established at St Thomas's Abbey at Dublin but they were further influential as colonials through their priories at Leixlip and Celbridge, Co. Kildare, at Newtown-Trim, County Meath, and at Bridgetown, County Cork. King Henry died in 1189 but the strategy which he instigated may be discerned even in matters appertaining to how the Victorines houses were to be thus located. He was followed in these matters by King John.

Outside of the areas where there was no great element of Hiberno-Norse in the population, dedications depended largely of course on the particular inclination of the new colonial magnates towards their own personal patron saints. The success of the priories they introduced was often regarded only with the ease with which members of the magnate's family could be accommodated with "posts" of Abbot, Prior, Abbess or other Superior in the priories founded within the districts they had carved out for themselves. Although the ability of the persons appointed would not have been deemed great, many proved successful.

---

[17] From the beginning FitzClare (Strongbow) founded Kilmaiham for The Hospitallers (1178). FitzAudelin did the same at St. Thomas's Abbey for the Augustinian canons (Archbishop Laurence O'Toole laid the foundation stone for it in 1172). 18 new houses for the Cistercians and Benedictines, 16 for the Augustinian canons and 4 for canonesses were founded within a short period (**See Prof Otway-Ruthven's** *A History of Medieval Ireland* (London 1968) p.127)

Katherine Lewis and others have been able to portray church events, internal politics and developments on a much broader canvas for England than has been possible for Ireland. Such matters were better documented in England. Saint Katherine's name occurs quite often. Good evidential material is available there also for cities, towns, abbeys, priories and churches. There are many records of bequests under wills and the names appear of chant-chapels in Saint Katherine's honour. These together with sponsors, and charters granted by wealthy magnates and other promoters abound. In Ireland by contrast the surviving sources are meagre; nevertheless it is both possible and worthwhile to explore what is known of the saint and the evolution of her cult in a specifically Irish context. Scholars researching the post Anglo-Norman period for Ireland from other perspectives have also provided useful material and much more is to be hoped for.

Some Religious aspects of the Anglo-Norman Invasion of Ireland.

The antagonism of many of the clerics who came to Ireland in this period to Ireland towards their Irish monastic confreres has been remarked upon in some histories. The new Orders of monks, canons and nuns were clearly trained to inculcate better practises in the native clerics they were to come across. The lay Lords, of course, brought their own religious people, in the first instance for the purpose of providing services for themselves and the settler families joining with them. Some were surprised to find a fairly well organised Church already in place though in scattered monastic towns of a type they were not used to in England or France.

For a time, without the Irish language to communicate with, they assumed they were dealing with a low level of culture even if the native clergy did have a smattering of Latin. The settlers were not too sure how to deal with them at first, a few for a rather lengthy period taking an antagonistic approach.[18]

---

[18] For one such mention, see **Michael A.Murphy** in RV(1915) where he refers to the foundation of the monastery of Cahir. Co. Kerry in 1491" under the express condition that no one but an Englishman should be admitted to make his profession there. This condition was by no means uncommon in the foundation charters of several Anglo-Irish monasteries. By the Norman Founders a systematic bycott of Irish monks was carried out.. The Norman Church was in Ireland a political institution and its monasteries were outposts against the Irish". Prof. **Otway-Ruthven**, on the other hand considers racial conflict was not a factor. See pp.29-30 of her *History* (London 1968), perhaps referring to the earliest phase.

The operation of the Brehon Law proved a stumbling block as it permitted many things that were anathema to the settlers and vice versa. The chieftains could speak for their tribes but had no unified plan of action. That hostility was displayed by the newly arrived ecclesiastics is hardly surprising given that many of the leading abbots' ideas were formed through contact with crusaders returning to England/France. These early religious, influenced in their thinking by laymen having had experience in the Holy Land, sometimes forgot that their informants had been dealing with heathens. Presenting themselves this time as 'Christianising' collaborators along with the hardy settlers they had brought them was unfortunate as it introduced elements conducive of conflict. The lay people were focused upon proceeding with an invasion using force if necessary, while at the same time the religious were expected to serve the spiritual needs of natives who seemed to them, with their Brehon Laws etc, only partially converted pagans.[19] Utilising their own religious preferences as an adjunct to conquest may have seemed to them perfectly legitimate, not to say praiseworthy.[20]

As we have seen above, and will in still more detail later, the Victorines were a congregation of canons regular having received instructions from the highest Angevin (Plantagenet) Royalty on how to proceed. One piece of advice they received and posited in this present essay, was to utilise the cult of Saint Catherine, (which they may not have hitherto espoused) in order to bring over the divergent Irish to a continental type ethos. As already indicated, the early 'Catherine 'abbeys were clearly sited in lands where many Ostmen were congregated.

The legend of Saint Catherine relates that at the moment of Saint Catherine's execution a voice was heard to declare 'Heaven's gates are open to you and to those who will celebrate the passion with devout minds.'The wide acceptance of this dictum amongst the Irish explains perhaps her great appeal, Many in distress under aggressive land appropriations were to turn to her as a sure refuge in difficult times and to accept their lot compliantly, (perhaps not the outcome expected by the escheators of their former lands.) Others, not heeding the legend, turned to forceful resistance.

---

[19] For a summary of the history of this period and the Anglo-Norman Colonisation see **Robin Frame's** *Colonial Ireland 1169-1369* (Dublin 1981) also for later times, Rolf Loeber's pamphlet *English Colonisation in Ireland 1534-1609 (Athlone 1991)*

[20] See **H.S.Sweetman** (Ed.) *Calendar of Documents Relating to Ireland 1171-1251* (London 1875) for the popes congratulatory epistle to King Henry II on his triumph over the Irish, exhorting him to remove their abominable practices and to recall them to worship of Christian faith. The original in Latin is to be found in *Pontificia Hibernica* Vol.1 p.19

Undoubtedly the administration of the newly acquired Irish lands by the Anglo-Normans in the thirteenth century was remarkably effective, that is to say without taking any account of their intervention in the field of religion. Without this their easy success is rather unexpected. Canterbury (meaning the Archbishop and his monks there) was anxious to reassert former claims to jurisdiction in Ireland. The great Benedictine Archbishops of Canterbury in the eleventh century, Lanfranc (d.1089) and Anselm (d.1109) had assumed that, as Ireland had anciently been converted from Britain, they had a prescriptive right to Primacy over the two islands. The Irish bishops felt forced at that time to call a national Synod (that of Rath Breasail (1111) from which they sent a request to Rome to be supplied with their own Irish primate together with provincial archbishops.[21]

After some politicking (it took Rome a while to move but) eventually in 1152 Pope Eugenius III(1145-1153) officially excluded Canterbury from primacy over the Irish Church by granting that honour instead to Armagh. When Henry II noted there was official approval and papal backing for Anglo-Norman colonisation of Ireland from a Bull from a later Pope, Adrian IV (1154-1159) and again from his contemporary Pascal III (1168-1178) Canterbury's interest was suddenly reawakened. King Henry was not hesitant in assuming control over the Irish chiefs. Receiving the further support of a still sympathetic papacy (under Pope Alexander III) and following the success of Strongbow at arms, new life was given to Canterbury's hopes of primacy over a Church of the two islands and the invasion was embarked upon by Strongbow and friends, quite obviously with Anglo-Norman Church approval (some Saxon bishops dissenting)

The promotion in Dublin, Cork, and Waterford of the cult of a saint popular in England and France seems hardly to have amounted to much more than a quietly calculated strategy. Its arrival in those localities (after a little manoeuvring by the King himself) must be considered of some significance. The aforesaid canons from Bristol and its environs (and almost certainly from Paris and other parts of Normandy) were sent to Ireland evidently at the King's request for the purpose of serving in abbeys dedicated to Saint Catherine. He had for some time being

---

[21] See for instance, **Martin Holland** in his *Dublin and the Reform of the Irish Church in the 11th and 12th centuries* in *Peritia* 14 (Turnhout 2000) also Chapter 1 of **Flanagan** (Oxford 1989). A wide-ranging general account of the subject is Prof. **David Bethell's** *English Monks and Irish Reform in the 11th and 12th centuries* in *Historical* Studies VIII (Dublin 1971) The pamphlet by **J.D.Seymour** *The Twelfth Century Reformation in Ireland* (Dublin 1932) is useful for Canterbury and the Irish Church

preparing them for this project and presented the Anglo- Norman canons as proteges of the Archdeacon of Bath. The latter person had been subtly prepared for taking over the archbishopric of Dublin.[22]

While living for a time with his mother the "Empress" Matilda in Bath/Bristol as Count of Anjou, the young Prince Henry was impressed by the Benedictines there (He had been educated at Chartres). It is not unlikely that he was the instigator of the migration from his French dominions of some of the Victorine canons that had settled in the Counties of Somerset and Gloucestershire, i.e. in the seventies of the twelfth century.[23]

The Benedictines were followers of Saint Catherine and possessed some relics of hers at Rouen. They greatly influenced the Victorines who in return followed many Benedictine practices in their canonries. It appears probable that King Henry may have wished to dedicate the new Benedictine Abbey he proposed for the Liberties of Dublin to Saint Catherine but following the murder in the Cathedral at Canterbury of the Archbishop, Thomas a'Beckett, (1170) he was forced to abandon the idea and instead dedicated it to Saint Thomas, the martyred Archbishop, in order to mollify the pope. The leaders of the king's religious mission to Ireland whom he was. However, to call on were not the Benedictines but the said Congregation of Saint Victor of the Canons Regular of Saint Augustine.[24] It must be remembered that Henry was very much French in ethos and the dedication of the Abbeys to Saint Catherine would been intended to favour the Ostmen who were so much part of the Dublin of the time. But other needs supervened.

---

[22] The account given in the foregoing is drawn from the general histories and from the works of **Father Gwynn**. These authorities would not agree the canons of Saint Victor were present in Ireland before ca. 1190. This present writer believes they came during the lifetime of Henry II. It is probable that the Parish of Saint Catherine in Dublin was in existence in some form previous to 1170, being in Ostman territory

[23] During the civil war with King Stephen. 1142 - 1148, the Empress Matilda made her stand in Somerset and Gloucester but left for Normandy, in 1148 only to return with her eldest son, Henry at the age of 20, to claim his throne upon the death of Stephen in 1154 (**T.F.Tout's** *Advanced History of Great Britain (London 1906)* (The other Matilda, Stephen's Queen, founded The Royal Hospital of Saint Katherine at the Tower of London. etc. She was a famous devotee of Saint Catherine's)

[24] See **Elizabeth M Hallam's** *Henry II as a founder- of Monasteries* In *Journal Ecclesiastical History 23* (London 1979) pp. 122-5 This writer mentions his encouragement of monasteries to set up in England from Normandy and the Empress's influence bearing on the matter. Henry was instrumental himself in founding the Carthusian monastery of Witham in Suffolk If the canons sent to Ireland were England recruited it was neccessaeily after only a short novitiate. In the twelfth century, however there there was a great increase in the numbers of monastic houses in France- some of the communities becoming out of all proportion- and priors would have been glad to release some of their monks/canons to Ireland, **H. Peltier's** paper in *Revue du moyen age latin 11*(1946) p.32 is relevant.

CHAPTER 4

The Victorine Canons (1)

At the end of the twelfth century, several priories/abbeys of the Augustinian Canons Regular of the Victorine congregation were founded in Ireland or rather some were placed in houses that were already built, such as St Thomas's. The congregation of canons of this Order is to be distinguished, from their Aroassian brethren who had been introduced to Ireland by Saint Malachy in the 1140s at the instigation of his friend, Saint Bernard of Clairvaux. The Aroassian congregation in Ireland, while sometimes existing side by side with the Victorines, were however very different in outlook and compliance. **PJ Dunning** in his analysis of the Canons Regular of Saint Augustine in Ireland[25] noticed, (without remarking at all on their distribution), that the Victorines were the handmaidens of the Anglo-Normans while the Aroassians remained aloof. The latter continued to adhere to the scheme of self - reformation enjoined upon the Irish Church by the twelfth century synods. The granting of the pallium by the pope in 1152 to the archbishop of Armagh was, for them, definitive. **Evelyn Bolster** in her *History of the Diocese of Cork*[26] for instance, gives an account of a serious conflict between the canons of the Aroassian Order of Gill Abbey and those of the Victorines of the Abbey of Saint Catherine in that city. Their cultural affinities were quite distinctive and remained so for centuries. In the following survey, in cases where monastic institutions both within and without the Pale are stated to be favourable to the colonists they will often be assumed Victorine and not Aroassian.

Known priories of the Victorines in Ireland were located at Saint Catherine's parish in Thomas Street, Dublin, (that is the Abbey of Saint Thomas the Martyr), Saint Catherine's Abbey Leixlip, County Kildare, Saint Wolstan's Priory, Celbridge, County. Kildare, Saint Catherine's Abbey, Waterford, Saint Catherine's Priory at Shandon in Cork, Saint Mary's Abbey in Bridgetown County Cork, Saint Mary's Priory at Newtown next Trim, County Meath, at an almost forgotten Priory at Callan Co. Kilkenny and a similar but mere offshoot of St Thomas Court - Saint John's near Enniscorthy, County Wexford. At various times the Victorines also had houses (or installed canons in them) at Mothel and Molana, County Waterford, and Muckamore Co. Antrim also very probably at Nook, County

---

[25] See Rev. **P.J. Dunning.** *The Arroasian Order in Medieval Ireland* in *Irish Historical Studies* (iv) (1945) pp 297 -315. Also see **Sarah Preston's** unpublished PhD Thesis (TCD) The *Canons Regular of Saint Augustine in Medieval Ireland*

[26] See **Sr.Evelyn Bolster.** *A History of the* Diocese of Cork Part 1, (Shannon 1972) p.224 where, a full account of the Victorines in Cork appears.

Wexford. (and, in equal probability, at Kells, County Meath and Callan, Co. Kilkenny as will be shown below). Furthermore the Community of Saint Victor were closely associated with the nunnery of Saint Catherine de O'Conyl, near Foynes, County Limerick. Allusion will be later made to a few other sites with which they were probably connected but for which there is inadequate supporting evidence to claim patronage or association. It will be pointed out that some foundations bore dedications other than to Saint Catherine.

Few remains of built structures exist today, even in a very ruined state, to testify to the former presence of the canons, powerful as they once had been. The ruined Bridgetown Priory is the most substantial remnant, though it, too, is now in poor condition. The ruins at Newtown-Trim are dwarfed by the equally ruined former Cathedral beside it (This may mean the priory was absorbed by the Cathedral shortly after the new diocese of Meath was formed early in the thirteenth century) The new Cathedral, having its own canons, came not long after the Victorines arrived. It is fair to assume there was then an exodus of the Victorines, or a large number of them, being French. They were sent to Bridgetown. Perhaps they were adept at building large structures, going when the Cathedral at Newtown neared completion.

County Meath has also an enigmatic site at Oristown bearing Saint Catherine's name. The ruined church there is thought to date from late twelfth or early thirteenth century. The presence of Saint Catherine's name may, here as elsewhere, give rise to a suspicion of Victorine association. There does not appear, however to be an Ostman connection to the area although an attack made on a De Lacy castle built in Kells, outside the Pale, in 1178 was made by an army of Dublin Ostmen. There may have been small settlements along the Boyne and Blackwater yet to be discovered by archaeology (which would not be surprising).

It has not been possible to discern a Victorine connection with Killybegs though there was probably a distant one with Lough Derg, County Donegal to be discussed below. (Some of these sites will receive further treatment later). Ruins of a medieval convent near Foynes, County Limerick dedicated to Saint Catherine, are neglected and rarely visited, as has been stated,but, a connection has been found with Saint Catherine's Abbey Waterford, through Keyn)sham Abbey in Somerset. [27/ 28]

---

[27] It is likely the builders of Waterford Courthouse made use of what remained of the old abbey's stonework. At the time, according to **Fr. Butler,** (see next note) some Augustinian Hermit Friars, occupied a habitable part of it in the eighteenth century and were ejected.

[28] **See Fr. Thomas C. Butlers** *John's Lane* (Dublin 1983) which contains a useful summary of Irish ecclesiastical matters appertaining to the later medieval period in Ireland.

Figure No.6. Waterford Courthouse today, at Catherine Street
(It is located directly on the former site of the medieval Abbey of Saint Catherine)

Figure No.7. From a water-colour by Doug Patterson (2001)
"The Church of the Transfiguration, Bell Tower and Minart at the Monastery
of Saint Catherine at Mount Sinai" (Courtesy of Saint Catherine Foundation
London, Geneva and New York)

Saint Catherine's cult in Western Europe

The series of steps whereby the cult of Saint Catherine came to Europe has been examined by **Katherine J. Lewis** in her book. She places the emergence of the cult in Normandy in the eleventh/twelfth centuries. Her tracing of the progress of the cult in England from 1100 onwards is useful. It is supplemented by a lecture given by **Christine Walsh** on *The Role of the Normans in the Development of the Cult of St Katherine.*[29]

It seems impossible to achieve a connected narrative of the cult's progress in Ireland, dependant as it is mostly on surviving dedications to the saint or, even where these may be absent, upon chance survivals of figure sculpture depicting St Catherine's wheel or sword device. Where her name survives at all it may be in a street name or Ordnance Survey reference (1829-1840) to a lost Holy Well or to an old graveyard mound. Often these may be passed by with hardly a moment's thought until enquiries are made in the locality. In the case of a few parishes that have not retained the name of Saint Katherine of Alexandria in either full or contracted form, the original cult may occasionally be confirmed by devotions taking place on her Feast Day.

---

[29] A lecture delivered at. the International Medieval Congress, Leeds 1999

Many dedications have undoubtedly been lost over the centuries in areas early colonised by the Anglo-Normans. During the Suppressions of the sixteenth century officials who might have usefully recorded artefacts often did not do so from an antipathy to a sainthood especially if approved by the pope. Still later, churchmen may have been reluctant to continue to accept a somewhat doubtful Egyptian-saint, and/or have had a preference for one of the other Saint Katherine's (of Sienna, of Laboure, of Sweden, etc.) Other saints even if dissimilar in name having a feast near the same day as hers might sometimes deprive Saint Catherine of her rightful place. (It seems possible, for instance, that an obscure Saint James 'Incercisus' may have partially succeeded in doing that at, Ramsgrange, and Dublin His survival as a joint patron may be accounted for by his being confused with one of the better known James such as the apostles of the same name. Intercisus was another favourite of Metaphrastes. His Feast day is 24th November, the day before Saint Catherine's.

Hospitals and Lazar Houses.

All of Europe suffered from plagues as well as famines during the Middle Ages. The charitable duty to render aid to the dying and support for the resulting orphans devolved upon the religious houses. There were several institutional "hospitals" in Ireland but only in a rather indistinct record. It is tempting to wonder if the name of Saint Catherine for some of them has not disappeared in the blur.[30] For the granting of patronage to hospitals the incoming settlers from England's south-east would have had the example of the great Saint Catherine's Hospital by the Tower of London. This was very famous and many would have wished to copy the same dedication and plan. Some ruined monastic sites may be mistaken for such and the name lost. Again, prayers to the saint in supplication of her aid in sickness were offered for many of the better off at altars where her name would have been revered. In England Dedicatory altars were common in medieval times, though relatively much less so in Ireland (See below under 'Others' p.111 for those noted)

---

[30] Many townland names contain the element "hospital", (2 No.) or the Irish "spiddal/spittal". (15 No.) while the words "lobhar" and "othar" (=the sick) abound in names of places where patients gathered for relief (or perhaps indicating lost hospital sites).

Effigies of Saint Catherine have survived in Ireland especially on the tombs of wealthy women: She is identifiable by her defining wheel, and occasionally by her palm of oratory or sword of martyrdom or both—the sword shown pointing downwards (See illustrations in **John Hunt's** Vol. II (Dublin 1974). The importation of alabaster figurines of Catherine from the Bristol area was a busy trade before the reign of Henry VIII.[31] She was also patron of scholars (arising from the story of her overcoming the objections of the philosophers) also of seafarers, especially navigators. (considered a 'learned' profession) and librarians. Saint Catherine has given her name to several headlands in Scotland and the Isle of Wight. She is to this day the patron of students in their study halls amongst the Dominican and the Augustinian Orders of friars.

The elimination of Saint Katherine of Alexandria from the Calendar of the Church by the Holy, Office of the Vatican in 1969,[32] may not yet be the blow once expected for the popularity of her cult. Wherever devotions are solidly established already, permission to set up new Solemnities does not have to be sought from Rome.

Important centres for the Saint Catherine cult on the mainland continent were in the canton of Van in Switzerland, Jaen and Girona in Spain, Verona in Italy and Magdeburg in Germany, (where a relic of her finger is kept.) She was revered also amongst the Christians of Goa in India. Other saints have themselves patronised the Virgin and Martyr, Saint Catherine of Alexandria, in their prayers. Notably these were saints whose lives were amongst the Dominican Order either as a tertiary, such as St Catherine of Siena, of Italy, or as a Lay Brother like St Martin of Porres of Peru (St. Joan of Arc who was not an Order member but is important in that she claimed to have received visions, conversing with Saint Catherine, while her prophecies were admitted as possibly true at her trial.)

---

[31] For this and a summary of Saint Catherine's cult's impact on Ireland see **Catriona MacLoed's** several articles in the Journal of the *Royal Society of Antiquities of Ireland* especially: *Mediaeval Wooden Figure in Ireland*. 'The Kilcorban *St. Catherine and Calvary Figures)* Vol LXXV Part 4 (1945) and *Medieval Figure Sculpture* in *Ireland in the Holy Ghost Hospital Waterford* VOL LXXVI Part 2 (1946) {These latter statues are now on display in Waterford City Council Museum "The Granary". One is illustrated at Figure 20b. For medieval sculpture of Saint Catherine in Ireland generally see **J.Hunt & P. Harbison's** *Irish MedievalFigure Sculpture 1200-1600. 2 vols.* (London 1973/ 1974) hereinafter referred to as *'Hunt'* (1973-74)

[32] The Calendar of Saints revision was issued by Decree of the Sacred Congregation of Rites on March 21st 1969 and approved by the Pope for coming into force on 1st. January 1970. An article in *L'Osservatore Romano* by Rev. **Annebale Bugnini** appeared later explaining that the diminishing of some saints for historical reasons did not mean local celebrations were prohibited.

Saint Katherine of Siena was evidently named in baptism after the saint from Alexandria. She was her patron all during her life. She refers to her intervention in a difficult conversion in one of her letters to Father Delle Vigne (The letter is extant). This remarkable saint relates how she persuaded a condemned man (Nicholas Toldo), a serious criminal, to pray to Saint Catherine of Alexandria. He repented before his beheading.

Saint Martin of Porres declared on his death-bed he was being assisted by Saint Catherine of Alexandria. He is a popular saint of the Dominican Order.

The well known firework "The Catherine Wheel" became popular in the seventeenth century in England when celebrations began after the discovery of the Gunpowder Plot and the arrest of the Catholic Guy Fawks when trying to blow up the British Houses of Parliament. Where permitted by law today the whirling firework still crackles and bangs in England on the 5th November throwing out sparks. In Ireland it sometimes appears on Halloween, its origins being quite forgotten. Whoever gave it its popular name must have been well aware that, somewhere near at hand preparations were being made for the Feast of Saint Catherine in three weeks or so, the saint who was harrowed on the wheel.

Figure No.8. Tomb-slab from Jerpoint Abbey (Cistercian) Co. Kilkenny
(Photo Courtesy Duchas The Heritage Council)

Figure No.9. The Holy Monastery of Saint Catherine, Mount Sinai

CHAPTER 5

The Life

According to the *Catholic Encyclopedia* (1917 Edition)

"Of noble birth and learned in "When only eighteen years old Catherine upbraided the Emperor Maximius for persecuting Christians and for the worship of false gods. Astounded at the young girl's audacity., the tyrant detained her in his palace and summoned [fifty] scholars to cause her to apostatise. But she emerged from the debate with them, victorious. Several even declared themselves Christians and were at once put to death. Maximius thereupon had Catherine scourged and imprisoned. The Empress herself went to visit her in her dungeon, and believing, straight away was herself martyred. Catherine soon afterwards effected so many conversions she was condemned to torture at the wheel, but at [an angel's] touch, this instrument was miraculously destroyed., the flying parts killing many. The enraged Emperor then had her beheaded. Angels,(or some say a group called 'Angeli') carried her body to Mount Sinai where later a church and Monastery were built in her honour."[33]

Saint Catherine's martyrdom, based on accounts of the reign of Maximius, is thought to have taken place sometime about AD 303 to 311. The Life also refers to a miraculous marriage with Christ himself, this section appearing, perhaps, to be based on a supposed reconstruction of the saint's name from the Greek[34]. (This formation, however, does not seem to apply in dedications to Mary, also a 'Blessed Virgin', resulting sometimes that her dedication maybe usurped by Catherine; the opposite is thought locally to have taken place at Mothel's Holy Well, County Waterford, which is located beside a ruined Victorine Priory. This Holy Well is dedicated to the Blessed Virgin along with a pattern for the Annunciation. It would rather be expected to have followed the patronage of Saint Catherine's Abbey Waterford from which the priory was founded.

---

[33] Taken from *The Catholic Encyclopedia* (London 1907) The 1986 edition is unnecessarily dismissive For critical evaluation of "The Legend" see **Hyppolyte Delahay's** *The Legends of the Saints* (Dublin 1995 Reprint)and **Rt.Rev.F.G. Holbeck's** *The biographical Dictionary of the Saints* (London 1924) Donald Attwater in his *Saints' Lives* (Harmondsworth 1985) describes some of the claims of the Life as "preposterous "There were of course several Lives, generally following the lines of *The Golden Legend* (see **Voragine** (Princeton 1993) For one in the Irish language see below footnote 111 and Appendix No. 2

[34] See *Chambers' Dictionary (London 1972)* p.1630 & **Maguire** (1920)

The Late Medieval Katherine Cult in Normandy and England

Katherine Lewis delved, for England, into the origins of the eleventh/twelfth century cult of Saint Catherine. (or 'Katherine' as she has the spelling, followed here mostly where **Lewis** is being cited). **Lewis** believes that the east- European cult of Saint Catherine, previously unknown in the west, was deliberately introduced to France and fostered for pecuniary reasons, namely, to help with defraying the cost of building the Cathedral of Rouen in Normandy by attracting pilgrims.

Christine Walsh, as does **K. Lewis,** recognises the attractiveness of the 'Legend of Saint Katherine'. She is not quite so fastidious, however as **Lewis** in exploring the origin of some relics of the saint which she reckons were brought from Mount Sinai to France by a disaffected monk of the famous Holy Monastery of Saint Catherine there. **Christine Walsh's** interpretation of the story is that the monk came seeking alms for his monastery bearing relics but did not return home and died at Trier. (Someone from Rouen, however, may have hijacked the relics he brought with him. The result was that the Cathedral at Rouen is now dedicated to the Holy Trinity and Saint Catherine—though she is not mentioned in the foundation charter).[35] The Egyptian monk, Symeon by name, was hailed as a saint because of reputed holiness and after his death Saint Catherine's cult came to enjoy considerable success especially, from the date of the completion of the Cathedral. (in about 1100). Some of the relics in question ended up at the Benedictine monastery of 'St.Catherine a la Trinite au Mont' near Rouen. **Christine Walsh**, argues indeed that there must have been some prior knowledge of the saint in the area of Rouen. She asserts that by the early twelfth century she was one of that general stock of saints who would have been known to at least some sections of Norman society. "if she had been too obscure and unknown her cult would have stood little chance of success"[36] This perception appears to be true for twelfth century occurrences of the cult in Ireland also. It is often difficult to define origins in many cases or to ascribe them with complete certainty only to the coming of the Anglo-Normans

---

[35] A small chapel in the Saint's honour survived the wartime destruction of Normandy. Stained glass windows depicting the saint have, however, not survived

[36] The Market Square which fronts the beautiful Cathedral at Rouen was the site of the burning at the stake of Saint Joan of Arc. Her unburned heart is preserved and venerated at the Cathedral. Saint Catherine was one of Saint Joan's voices. The prophetic ability she displayed resulted in her condemnation as a witch in 1430. (See **D.A.Fradi's** *Joan of Arc and the Hundred Years Wa*r (Westport, U.S. 2005)

As far as England is concerned, devotion to Saint Catherine coincided with the influx of the Normans to that country following the conquest of 1066 and was promoted thereafter by the many mainland continental priests who followed the Conqueror., **Lewis** has traced the progression of the cult throughout England. For Ireland it is unlikely, that much was known about Saint Catherine (or Caitríona in the Irish language form) before 1169 except (speculatively) in certain Hiberno-Norse areas. When the first of the Anglo-Normans arrived, ecclesiastical historians have however demonstrated that there had been some interaction between the monastic orders of England and Ireland beforehand.[37] The Cistercian Order is a case in point. The monks of Llanthony in Wales also had a community at Duleek, County Meath from circa. 1160, not a rare example.[38] **A..F. O'Brien** has demonstrated the considerable influence of Rouen on Ireland through commercial relations in the eleventh and twelfth and centuries with ports along the south coast of Ireland from Wexford to Dingle[39] There is archaeological evidence for Rouennaise contacts with ports even farther afield in Ireland but particularly with Dublin. This activity continued still more strongly during the Anglo Norman period. (It seems inappropriate to surmise in this present essay, —as others have done— of a much earlier introduction of the cult directly, from Eastern Europe for which there is, however little good evidence)[40]

The results of the researches of **O'Brien** at Rouen and at southern coastal port sites in Ireland have been greatly supported by the new archaeological diagnostic finds of pottery at Dublin and elsewhere on the south and west coasts. There were also, it appears, beyond the commercial activity in the early period, lines of contact on religious matters between Ireland and Rouen and also with English towns on the Severn Estuary (notably Bristol). The Ostmen (the "Hiberno-Norse") of Dublin, Cork and Waterford maintained contacts by sea with sections of the population of Normandy and Aquitaine whose antecedents were also Viking[41] It may be concluded that Saint Catherine's cult was brought by several routes simultaneously, from England, and radiating roughly from Rouen and environs.

---

[37] See for example. **Gerard O'Brien 's** edition of **Rev. Aubrey Gwynn's** *The Irish Church in the 11th and 11th centuries* (Dublin 1992); also the latter's *Medieval Bristol* in *Irish Historical Studies (1947)*

[38] It is perhaps noteworthy that some of the Peter's Pence sent to Rome through London in 1154 may have been collected from Irish monasteries (i.e. other than Cistercian,) which were subject to Norman headship in England.

[39] See **A.F.O Brien's** *Commercial Relations between Aquitaine and Ireland ca.1000 and 1550'* in J.M. Picard (Ed).'s *Aquitaine and Ireland in the Middle Ages*; also **O' Brien's** contribution to **Nolan et al.** (Eds) *Cork History and Society* viz *The Cork and south Coast (1170-1583)*

[40] See **Canon Maguire** in his *History of the Diocese of Raphoe*. (Dublin 1921) Vol *(ii)* p.94. An extract of the relevant page is given in full as APPENDIX No.I p125

[41] See **Edmund Curtis's** *A History of Mediesel Ireland* 1110 to 1513 (London 1923) pp. 195 ff and Mary Valante's article *Dublin's Periphery in the later Viking* Age in Sean Duffy (Ed)*'s Medieval Dublin I* (Dublin 2000)

It is possible to identify a part of the city of Dublin where Rouennaise sailors used to congregate- the Cornmarket. Notable today is its Church, Saint Audoen's, dedicated to Saint Auen from Rouen. The other church in the neighbourhood, Saint Nicholas of Myra's,[42] is dedicated to a saint who also has Scandinavian antecedents ('adopted by the Danes') brought from northern France.

The Canons Regular of St. Augustine of the Congregation of Saint Victor ('The Victorines'), had their priories in England[43] clustered in the vicinity of Bristol to which city many of the new influences may be directly traced. For the Order **J.C.Dickinson** styles the following as English houses 'the chief being St.Augustine's Bristol, Wigmore, Wormsley, Worspring,[Woodspring] and possibly Keynsham and Stavordale, none very remote from Bristol'[44] **Father Aubrey Gwynn** in his paper on *The Early History of Saint Thomas's Abbey, Dublin* to the *Journal of the Royal Society of Antiquaries of Ireland,* (1954 Part I) (hereafter referred to as 'JRSAI') gives a good account of the "close ecclesiastical bonds between the Abbey of Saint Augustine. Bristol, and the Abbey of St. Thomas, Dublin', confirming at one point " further indication {s} of the connection between Bristol, Keynsham and Dublin"[45] **Gwynn** notes that the new (1181) 'Archbishop Cumin, successor of St. Laurence O'Toole., was conscious that "the canons of Saint Thomas's enjoyed the special favour of the Lord of Ireland". Previously the archbishop himself had been Archdeacon of Bath and a royal clerk before being nominated by the King to Dublin. (As prince Henry had known him in Bath). In this regard, it is also interesting that, according to **K Lewis,** it seems very likely Saint Catherine -was the patron saint of Bath. She says of an Oath Book used by the city "This life of St Katherine is the only saint's Life contained in the early fifteenth century "Red Book of Bath", attached to a chapel of 'St Katern' in the Church of St Mary de Stolls"[46]

---

[42] See **D.L. Canon** (Ottowa 2002)

[43] The Scandinavians of France were attached to this Saint. Known as 'the Danes Church') Interesting **David N. Duinville** points out that the Vikings who settled in the Confentin (Chenbourge) Peninsula were of mixed Scando-Gaelic culture (article in **Sean Duffy's** (Ed) *Medieval Dublin VI* (Dublin 2005) **Saint Nicolas** was patron of Norway jointly with **St. Olaf** from the 11th Century (See **D.L. Canon**, 2002 p148)

[44] 'See Rev. **J.C.Dickinson** *The Origin of the Austin Canons and their Introduction into England (London* 1950) p. 133. Wigmore in Herefordshire was founded directly from the Abbey of Saint Victoire in Paris.
See also **R.Dunning's** *Somerset Monasteries* (Stroud 2001).This gives 1172 as the foundation date for Keynsham. (Surely too late by many years?)

[45] For the early history of the abbey see **Rev Anthony Elliott's** *The Abbey of St. Thomas the Martyr near Dublin* in JRSAI (1892 Pt.I)

[46] See **Lewis** (2000) p.167 and the discussion therein following

N.B. Bristol and Bath are about 18 miles apart. Approximately midway is the town of Keynsham where stood the Abbey for Victorine Canons recently come to light through archaeology. After the Henrician Dissolution the Abbey fell into disrepair. In the 17th and 18th Centuries stone was carted away for the building of nearby towns and sadly the precious archives largely disappeared also. In Somerset, now part of the County of Avon, there are still to be found a Manor House and a Holy Well dedicated to Saint Catherine. There was a hospital dedicated to Saint Catherine at Bruton. **K Lewis** lists several churches in Somerset receiving bequests under 15th century wills requesting the saint's prayers. She mention Illmynstre, Wanstrow, St Ewans, Bristol &. Mary *de* Stall, Bath, Charde, Songsebury Etherptre, and others. The saint though evidently popular amongst Somerset people is not thought to have been special for the Victorines before arriving in Ireland as explained in the text.

CHAPTER 6

Friendship between the Augustinian (Aroassian) nuns of Clonard and the Grace Dieu canonesses of Lusk at the end of the twelfth century noted.

Besides the Victorine and Benedictine monasteries which were for men, there were other Orders for women. These included the Grace Dieu canonesses of Fingal (North County Dublin), the nuns of Clonard (from Counties Meath and Louth), the nuns of Kilcreevanty County Galway (Also 'The Black Nuns of O'Conyl', of County Limerick of whom special mention will be made below). **Gwynn and Hadcock** list over sixty convents of importance, nearly all following the Rule of St. Augustine. There are indications that several were patrons of Saint Catherine

The Grace Dieu canonesses (who are thought to have originated in Normandy) were also associated from mid-twelfth century within the Cornmarket area of Dublin. At some unknown date, probably after Strongbow's taking of the city, they came under the control of Saint Augustine's abbey in Bristol. Rouenaise sailors and merchants from northern France who had been used to congregate about Cornmarket, found lodgings there and sometimes settled permanently. When ejected by Strongbow in 1171 (as the site they occupied was to be included within the future walled city, and of course they were ethnically Hiberno-Norse), many of their people moved to Oxmantown on the north of the River Liffey and to Kilmainham to the west but the canonesses moved to the see- lands of the archbishop of Dublin in Fingal. There he at first presented them with some small holdings, adding to them later. Fingal was a district where there was a considerable settlement of Ostmen ('the Hiberno–Norse' of the historians) who were closely related to the people of Rouen and were familiar with their patois. The canonesses initially, it appears, received a new site at Portrane (where the local R.C. church of today is dedicated to Saint Catherine) They were given the use of a convent at Lusk offered to them as a temporary residence by the Aroassian (so called.'Clonard') 'nuns. The headhouse of the latter was in the town from which they received their name. (It subsequently removed to Odder)

The canonesses proceeded however, without delay, to build their own permanent head nunnery near Lusk. (The ruins of this are still to be seen just west of Blake's Cross, Lusk in the townland of Grace Dieu – behind the "Blooming Baskets" nursery.[47] The Grace Dieu nunnery, together with other sites belonging to the canonesses or under their control (at Portrane, Swords, Ballymadun[48] and presumably also, Fieldstown) became centres of education for the daughters of the landed gentry for three and a half centuries.[49]

It may be inferred from the frequent occurrence of accounts of and the name of Saint Catherine in the area, that these nuns were also instrumental in providing houses of religion throughout the area of what is now North County Dublin/Fingal. Along with the nuns of Clonard, they were the principal female order of the area. (The Clonard nuns, though supported by the dioceses of Meath and Clogher as well as the archbishopric of Dublin were probably less favoured in the Pale because of their Irishness). Several substantial grants of land came the way of the Grace Dieu nuns however between the thirteenth and sixteenth centuries and at the Henrician Dissolution are recorded as being in possession of one of the largest land-holdings in the area.[50] The Aroassian nuns of Clonard who had befriended them at Lusk, seemed not to mind their territories overlapping. (See the account of Saint Doulagh's church below) It may be that following the same Rule, and having the same patron saint contributed to their friendship.

---

[47] See the pamphlet *Short Histories of Dublin Parishes Part XVI* by **Bishop N Donnelly** (Dublin reprint nd.). He states "there was an altar in Lusk church dedicated to Saint Catherine "p 93. **Bishop Donnelly** gives a personal account of Grace Dieu at pp. 97/98.

[48] There is a record of Archbishop of Dublin (Henry of London) granting the church of Ballymadun and the titles of Palmerstown next Clonmethan to the nuns of Grace Dieu. See **E.St John Brook's** *The Irish Chartularies of Llanthony Prima and Secunda* (Dublin 1953 pp. ixx, xx)

[49] **Constantinia Maxwell** (1923) in her *Irish History from Contemporary Sources* p.127 gives the text of a protest to the King against the Henrician Dissolution of the Grace Dieu Order because of the loss of "the nunnery to gentlemen's children and others - being brought up in... learning... and in the English tongue and behaviour". **Hall** (2003) at p.175n gives further details, confirming the value of these nuns property at the Dissolution exceeded that of any other convent.

[50] See map accompanying **Prof. J Otway-Ruthven's** article *The Medieval Church Lands of County Dublin in Medieval Studies* (Dublin1961) Very small holdings do not appear in it but are referred to in **N.B.White** (1943) pp 58,68,74,77 which refers to gardens in the parish of Saint Katherine and in Saint Katherine Street, 80 acres at 'Newton,' a Cottage at Stradbally (beside Fieldstown),the Rectory of Ballymadun (a special grant of archbishop of Dublin) and another at Crumlin,—' a rectory of the parish church of' Saint Katherine in the Suburbs' (It may have been at Harold's Cross which seems to have been at one time in The Parish of Saint Catherine.)

Figure No. 10. The Church of Saint Catherine of Alexandria, Meath Street, Dublin. (R.C) (drawing by J. OHanlon)

INTERLUDE NO. 1

The earliest mention of Saint Catherine in a native Irish context occurs in the manuscript Calendar of Gorman, for which **Whitley Stokes**, the editor, proffers a date of 1164 to 1170[51]. The little verse therein where the name of 'Caitríona' occurs for the 25th November is in Middle Irish. This is consistent with the theory that the cult of Saint Catherine spread to Ireland through contact with France even before the colonising Anglo-Normans arrived. **Stokes** thinks that Abbot Gorman obtained his information from a Calendar of Saint Jerome. Interest in non-Irish saints largely ceased, except for Anglo-Saxon and apostolic ones, after the tenth century. **O Riain** believes O Gorman mined **M. Tallaght** (ninth century) but existing copies of the latter do not have November in which Saint Catherine's Day occurs. It may be presumed that she was popular with the small group of settlers from Rouen who lived in greater Dublin and the Grace Dieu nuns retained a connection with them. The coincidence of times seems significant.[52]

The monastic town of Louth, where abbot Gorman's scriptorium was located at Knock, was at that time in the then diocese of Clogher. Louth church was its nominal cathedral. Clonard was in County Meath not far from Trim and was the head house of the 'Clonard Nuns'. The nuns had several other convents in the Pale (Dulleek, Kells, Kilbride, Louth, Odder and Termonfeckin being the more important). Louth was located in an area in dispute between the Clogher and Armagh dioceses. That was over whether "the area lying between Carlingford and the River Boyne" should not be in Armagh diocese.

---

[51] See **Whitley Stokes** *Feilire Uí Chormain* (London 1895.

[52] But see **J.Hennig** *Non-irish saints in Feilire Oengusso. R.LA.* (1975)
There was considerable interest amongst ninth century calendarists in Ireland of non Irish saints -but evidently not in Saint Catherine. Her Feast. Day was taken from her (?) by Joannes Cassian in *Feilire Oengusso.*

The Clonard nuns certainly knew of Saint Catherine. A Holy Well for the saint is not far from Termonfeckin,[53] which also lay within the disputed area.referred to. They were also at Saint Doulagh's in Fingal where there is a Holy Well dedicated to the saint. (This church, though in the archdiocese, was under control of the Clonard nuns') So it seems that Saint Catherine may be numbered amongst the devotional saints of both communities i.e. at a time just contemporary with the arrival of the Anglo-Normans. The Clonard nuns were at Louth, (the site of Gorman's Monastery. This would suggest that the nuns and canonesses might have been together instrumental in the inclusion of Saint Catherine's name in **Gorman's** *Calendar* perhaps hiscalling on St.Jerome's calendar merely for confirmation of her existence.

It is thought that the scriptorium of the monastery of Knock near Louth is where the Annals of Ulster were compiled and consigned to the written word.

---

[53] Near Ardee - See **Larry Conlon's** article *the Holy Wells of County Louth* Part 2 in *Journal of the County Louth Archaeological and Historical Society* (Drogheda 2000)

CHAPTER 7

The Victorine canons (2.)
Saint Catherine's Abbey, Waterford a prime centre of the cult.

The Victorine canons' rule was based on the Augustinian but was more ascetic than that of the Aroassians, the usual community· of canons who followed the rule in Ireland up to ca. 1174. The former Order took- its name from the monastery of St. Victor at Paris which, according to **Dickinson**, was taken over in 1140 by a breakaway group of Benedictines under the influence of Bishop Ivo of Chartres which monastery it later outshone for scholarship. Both communities, however, continued to coexist in England in the twelfth century, the Victorines, being much favoured by the Empress Matilda, mother of the future king, Henry II.

The Abbey of St. Thomas the Martyr (Murdered 1170) at Dublin is said to have been founded in 1173 on behalf of the Royal Family. The appearance of the Victorine Order is not recorded in Ireland until the Prior of Waterford witnessed a Deed in 1202. They arrived the same year at Bridgetown, County Cork.and Newtown-Trim, County Meath. The Order must be presumed to have been at Waterford some years earlier.[54] From certain references it may be concluded that they were in Dublin by 1180. Their priories in Somerset were the source of the main supply of canons regular.

This being very early in their growth as a distinct community in Somerset must mean the Royal family were personally involved in the direction being taken by a mission evidently underway in association with the Benedictine monks who had preceded them in Waterford and Cork. These were the Victorines. They were also enclosed. followed many Benedictine practices, silences and so on and were probably for a while indistinguishable from them. There were strong bonds with the Benedictines of Bath, near-neighbours of the Victorine abbey of Keynsham which was in the diocese of Bath.

---

[54] **Maurice P. Sheehy** in *Pontificia Hibernicap*. 143 suggests the priory was founded by the Ostmen of Waterford and if this be so it may, indeed, have been considerably earlier but equally is consistent with the Gallo-Norse connection predicated in this article for all the 'Saint Catherine' Abbeys. **Mac Cotter** *Journal of the Kerry Archaelogical and Historical Society* (2004) gives Elias Fitz Anthony as founder. He was an Anglo Norman of unknown origin but probably French.

It is clear that Keynsham formed with the other Somerset abbeys a central reservoir of canons from which the three 'Saint Catherine' abbeys of Waterford, Leixlip and probably Cork drew. Saint Thomas's Abbey - Dublin also drew from Keynesham, but indications point to their not being the first canons there but came shortly after its dedication which was prominently declared to be that of the recently sainted archbishop of Canterbury. Eventually, within a very few years this abbey became itself the distribution centre for canons wherever they were needed in Ireland. There is an account of some being sent to Newtown-Trim and Bridgetown to make up shortfalls in the complement of Canons places, making one assume they were brought directly from Normandy since Keynesham was apparently founded no earlier than 1202 (**Dunning**)

The influence of the Hiberno-Norse or Ostmen

White in his *Extents* (1943) p.252-3 says that at the Dissolution there was a Farm at Dungarvan, Co. Waterford under Keynsham Abbey, which was evidently supplying produce to their houses in Waterford, Cork and elsewhere where they had ecclesiastical benefices (See **Mac Cotter** 2004) It has been noticed that all these places were within the Hiberno-Norse sphere of influence as placenames and other indicators show. The high incidence of Saint Catherine's name (with Waterford's) in these areas makes one think that the Royalty, Henry II and John, had the Victorine community in mind from early on to serve in Ostman territory. This they did for three hundred years.

As for the Benedictines, the adoption of their Rule widely by the various several other Orders was probably sufficient for them to leave the field wide open to the canons for the time being. Benedictine abbeys needed ample lands to remain viable, a fact which may have deterred the early Anglo-Norman magnates from founding or affording them. (It is noted by a correspondent to JRSAI (1912 that the Benedictine Priory of Waterford, a mere cell of Cork at the time, had failed because of "an exclusive and anti- Irish spirit".[55] Although many Irishmen traditionally travelled to the continental mainland to join the Order those at home who may have not been Irish looked down on the local members of their Order as somewhat 'barbarous') Also the canons could receive tithes and gifts whereas the Benedictines were not permitted to do so. Though they had several cells of influence, they had only two moderately sized Abbeys in Ireland.

---

[55] See **Dom Hubert B de Berebeke** *The Benedictines in Medieval Ireland* in JRSAI (1950 Part 1)

The Victorines' choice of 'Catherine' sites among the Ostmen is indeed notable. They seem to have been attracted to (or perhaps directed to) such locations as Leixlip-Lucan in County Dublin, as well as to Waterford and Cork. In all these places their abbeys or priories were located in twelfth century Ostman territory. It may therefore have not been merely coincidental that these houses were dedicated to Saint Catherine but rather her patronage may have come full circle in those areas.

The Abbey of St Thomas the Martyr in the Liberties of Dublin.

For Ireland the abbey of Saint Thomas the Martyr in Dublin- was probably considered, from King John's reign, to be the Victorines' head-house, though in practise it was independent. ('The Abbey - or some parts of it - were later to be called 'Thomas Court')[56] The site has been recently examined in detail and described, with a map and archaeology.[57] The Parish in which the old Abbey stood is called "Saint Catherine's". (As stated above, in combination with the adjoining one to form, 'The Parish of Saint Katherine and Saint James') Saint Catherine's name originated here, possibly with the arrival of some Norman, or Rouennaise clerics before 1170; thus preceding the dedication of the Abbey to Saint Thomas. A change of name is postulated. (An expedient move on the part of King Henry in 1171, following the martyrdom of the archbishop of Canterbury (in 1170) for which he was held partly to blame). It is permissible to conjecture then, that Dublin's abbey, like the house at Waterford, was first intended for dedication to Saint Catherine; but to be changed later at Dublin. At any rate the (pre Invasion) parish's dedication has continued, if not the Abbey's.

---

[56] The definitive article in the matter is **Rev Aubrey Gwynn's** in *JRSAI (1954) pt I*. There are further details in Rev..**Anthony Elliott's** *The Abbey of St.Thomas the Martyr near Dublin* in JRSAI (1892) pt I and **Gwynn's** article *Archbishop Cumin* in *Reportorium Novum Vol.1 No.1 (Dublin 1956) pp285* ff, In this last he notes the pope reprimanding the then Archdeacon Cumin forholding a quasi-lay post at Bath. This he had done for five years before coming to Dublin as archbishop.

[57] See **Claire Walsh's** *Archaeological excavations at the Abbey of St Thomas The Martyr, Dublin* in **Sean Duffy**(Ed.) *Medieval Dublin* Part 1 (Dublin 2000). (Contd.) The drawing (Figure No. 3 of this present article), shows the plan of the abbey site as it was in 1634. Permission for its reproduction and inclusion here is by courtesy of the National Library of Ireland.

The parish also incorporates the churches of Saint Catherine, Thomas Street and Saint Catherine's, Donore Avenue (formerly - "Saint Victor's"- both Church of Ireland) and Saint Catherine of Alexandria's Roman Catholic Parish Church, Meath Street. This last is also within the bounds of the parish of Saint Catherine. (though does not appear so in Crawford's map(1996 p.14). The civil parish is still more extensive, taking in much of the Liberties and extending into the Barony of Uppercross. The Earl of Meath, whose ancestor, Sir William Brabazon, received the grant of the St. Thomas Abbey at the Dissolution of 1538, and his descendants still own many of the ground rents. Only negligible traces of the once great abbey were found during the Archaeological Survey (1995). The survey was perforce limited in area to those places not since built upon or where no useful modern structures stood in the way. However it can be deduced that the Abbey Church of Saint Catherine was along the present Hanbury Lane in or about the Thomas Court Training Centre and Meath Market.[58]

The former Church of Ireland parish church, Saint Catherine's, Thomas Street, now the parish hall, recently received considerable media attention, in connection with its excellent refurbishment[59] The Roman Catholic parish church, Meath Street (Figure 10) was similarly feted in 1958 upon the centenary of its reconstruction It houses a fine marble statue of Saint Catherine at the High Altar. The present structure replaces an older church of 1858 which had been built in the form of an octagon representing Saint Catherine's wheel.[60] On each of the eight sides there was a fresco or window showing some facet of the saint's life.

---

[58] The church appears in the background of the painting *The Execution of Robert Emmett* (by **F.W. Byrne** in National Gallery of Ireland – See *The Irish Arts Review (Spring 2003)* It was hardly intended to replace the James Malton print but it has its own interest. *The* graveyard at the rear is now a public park maintained by the Dublin City Council - called 'Saint Catherine's Park'.

[59] A detailed account of the old church appears in *Reportorium Novum* (1959 – 60) p 395

[60] *See Pontificia Hibernica ii p.19*

Figure No. 11 Marble Statue of Saint Catherine at the High Altar of the Parish
Church of Saint Catherine of Alexandria, Meath Street, Dublin

CHAPTER 8

Other evidence for Saint Catherine's cult in Counties Dublin and Kildare
The no longer extant Saint Catherine's Abbey, Leixlip, Co. Dublin

Continuing the subject of Saint Catherine among the Ostmen, an obvious case requiring to be considered is the Priory of Saint Catherine of Alexandria, Leixlip, the very former existence of which is no longer to be seen on the ground.

The Ostmen, ('Hiberno-Norse) were settled in this area since the Battle of Clontarf (1014). In the district of Leixlip-Lucan under Anglo Norman dispensation, the Welsh grantee of the lands, (1204) Warisius de Peche, was encouraged to found an Abbey or Priory. He did so in 1219 (**Gwynn and Hadcock**) a date which seems late for a Victorine foundation— 30 years after the death of King Henry II. But Victorine it was. (Could it be that its existence had a purpose—in order to accommodate a new group of Victorines). Warisius had been granted the lands at his marriage to a granddaughter of Strongbow. A relative, John Warisius, became Prior. (One suspects a small surplus of canons at Keynsham were having to be placed somewhere. **Westropp** thought arrangements were often made "through some unexplained favour of the ruling powers to the Augustinian Abbot of Keynsham"). John was King at this time[61].

The priory of Leixlip (Saltus Salmorum in Latin) was sometimes referred to as 'Abbey') Upon its foundation it became very shortly appropriate to Saint Thomas's Abbey as if it had somehow failed, perhaps by the small number of canons there. It was eventually united to it in 1287 as a 'conventual dependency'. (**Gwynn and Hadcock** p.192). Together these communities should have been of great influence in working for the spiritual benefit of all the settlers in their chosen area. This included some of the Dublin Pale as well as districts on the banks of the Liffey where many of the older 'colonists', the Ostman, still remained (This was probably what king Henry had intended with his well known ability for thinking ahead. There were many Ostmen on record as rendering fealty to the king)

---

[61] See **Emer Purcell's** *The Expulsion of the Ostmen 1169-71 ;the documentary evidence* (in *Peritia 2003-2004*) for an account of the Dublin Ostmen and their survival.

Saint Thomas's Abbey had considerable tracts of land in the several other Pales, notably in County Cork. At Leixlip the present Hotel, 'St Catherine's Park', is situated in the very large townland of 'St. Catherine's' where there are left a few what appear to be fragmentary ruins from the old priory (See e.g. Figure No. 5). Otherwise little remains of anything related to the large priory once located there, of antiquarian interest today except for a group of Holy Wells one of which is dedicated to Saint Catherine as noted by **O Danachair**, the folklorist[62]

Saint Wolstan's Priory, Celbridge County Kildare.

From the start it became clear that the size of Saint Catherine's Priory at Leixlip made it too unwieldy for the relatively small number of canons there. Arrangements were instituted by the two great magnates who were possessors of the land together with the Abbot of Saint Thomas Court to divide it and thus make it somewhat easier to manage. Large endowments came to it without avail. The first steps were taken in 1287 when one large part was taken directly into the management of Saint Thomas Court, Dublin, a portion being annexed by the neighbouring Saint Wolstan's Priory and some going to Lucan Castle, (the residence today of the Italian Ambassador.)

This latter Priory had been dedicated to Wolfstan, the great saint of Worcester. Adam de Hereford who had arranged the foundation of Saint Catherine's Leixlip. He was a powerful individual and companion of Strongbow. He had been cured of the dropsy by the miraculous intercession of Saint Wolfstan. and wished to found a house in his honour. He had set aside the lands near Celbridge as early as 1205 for that purpose. He had been Strongbow's agent for many matters in Ireland, for instance setting up Warisius de Peche as Lord of Leixlip and Lucan. The monastic Order at Saint Catherine's Leixlip was that of Saint Victor the same as at Saint Thomas Court. There seems to have been some disagreement as to the authority of the prior of Saint Catherine's Leixlip, as the pope made him subservient to the Abbot of Saint Thomas's by Decree of 1238.[63]

---

[62] In a note on these Holy Wells in *Bealoideas* Iml X11 (1947) the writer seemed unaware of the former presence in their vicinity of an important Priory bearing the name of the same saint he wished to remark upon, but feels forced to invent a spurious account of her.

---

[63] **O'Donovan**, quoted in **Michael Herity** 's edition of *Ordnance Survey Letters- Kildare* (Dublin 2002)

The name of a certain William de Kavesham appears in the charter record (1271) for Saint Wolstan's priory, (presumably in error for' Keynsham '– he had been, after all, seneschal to the former Archbishop Cumin of Dublin, (d..1212) who came from the same area of Somerset. The current archbishop was Fulk de Sandford) William is mentioned as having given back in 1271 some lands which had been granted to him out of the estate of the Priory of Leixlip, (presumably as a further attempt at a reduction in the acreage under the prior's control).William had by doing this subverted the intended action by enabling some canons to stay on and continue to say masses for his own soul and those of his family on there anniversaries.[64]

As well as by the founder, Adam de Hereford, Saint Wolfstan was also patronised by King John. He died in 1216. Though a true Norman, John elected to be buried in the Anglo-Saxon Saint Wolfstan's chapel at Worcester.

Some Holy Wells of Dublin and County dedicated to Saint Catherine.

O Danachair's survey, *The Holy Wells of County Dublin,* published in *Reportorium Novum* (1957-8) lists and describes six wells dedicated to Saint Catherine in County Dublin (including Fingal). Of interest are several 'to whom devotion became popular in medieval times and continued later, some into the twentieth century. It is highly probable that we owe their [original] dedication to Norman-English influence.' **O Dannachair** notes. Three of the more important Holy Wells for Saint Catherine are discussed below:- one is in Grace Dieu townland, near the site of the former nunnery of the Order of the same name 'Grace Dieu'. This townland is a place where there are also Holy Wells dedicated to Saint Brighid, Saint Mary and Saint Macullian. These latter wells evidently resisted substitution of Saint Catherine's name even though nearby a onetime nunnery the members of which are presumed to have had great devotion to her This supposition is based upon their being an Order from Normandy where Saint Catherine's cult was general. It will, however be supported by an accumulation of facts soon to be related.

---

[64] From **John Dalton's** *History of the County of Dublin* (Dublin 1838)
In a recent article *Medieval Nunneries of the Irish Pale*, **Margaret MacCurtain** gives a good account of the Grace Dieu canonesses (at pp. 158 to 140 of the book *Surveying Ireland's Past*- the Festschrift in honour of Prof Annagret Simms (Dublin 2004)

Fieldstown Holy Well

One Holy Well, for which the dedication (plus 'rounds', 'a pattern', etc. are recorded as late as the early twentieth century is known as "Saint Catherine's Holy Well, Fieldstown". It is well documented. The Fieldstown lands were among those coming into the hands of the Barnewall family at the Henrician Dissolution of the monasteries (1538/40) The religious house there was one among a cluster of churches and their glebelands in close proximity to each other in the present parish of Rolestown (Fingal, County Dublin.)

At Fieldstown today is to be seen a mound and gravemarkers, evidence of the site having a once monastic settlement or church beneath. It is mentioned in documents of the Dissolution and charters of subsequent grants of lands preserved in muniment Registers. (See footnote 29). Located in the former Parish of Clonmethan, the lands belonged to the Augustinian canonesses of Grace Dieu. The chapel there was evidently of some importance though by the sixteenth century it is recorded as 'subservient to the church of Clonmethan.' The Holy Well on the site is dedicated to Saint Catherine and was much frequented in the past. The Patron Day was, as usual, celebrated on the 25th of November.

In 1521 Nicholas Dowdall, Prebendary of Clonmethan, in a petition
to parliament submitted:

> *"Divers persons, aliens, strangers and denizens, frequent in*
> *considerable numbers, by way of pilgrimage the chapel of*
> *Saint Catherine,Virgin and Martyr of Fieldstown, which was*
> *appropriated and annexed to the prebend of Clonmethan,*
> *being for the health and safety of their souls and accomplishment*
> *of their petitions and prayers. And these persons* [he complained]
> *had been repeatedly vexed and molested under divers pretences*
> *by reason of which they were obliged to lay aside said devotions*
> *and pilgrimages."*[65]

Father Dowdall was successful in his representations as parliament issued
the following:

> *"All on pilgrimage and those going there, dwelling there and*
> *returning, while behaving decently in the King's liege ......*
> *are granted the King's' protection while in progress.....*
> *in default of £20 to be exacted from any vexatious person."*
> [a very large fine for the time]

Recently efforts have been made at Oldtown to resurrect the pattern
but without success so far (2006).

---

[65] Mr **Charles MacNeill** *of* the Society of Antiquaries in their Journal for 1922 gives a report of a 16th century
sale of gold and silver and other jewels taken from "profane images at the chapel of St Katherine at Feld*stone"*
(that is during the Henrician Dissolution 1540). It lists the proceeds. Because of the Barnewall association with
Fieldstown, their connection with the Canonesses of Lusk may be taken as evident. About this time ca 1550,
Patrick Barnewall of Fieldstown was granted the then large village of Whitestown, the outlying parts of which
probably comprised the villages of Rush and Portrane as well (See **N.B. White** (1943) p.58

St. Doulagh's

Another significant Holy Well listed by **O Danachair** which is dedicated to Saint Catherine is that at Saint Doulagh's Church in the parish of Balgriffin on the road from Dublin to Malahide, a suburb of Dublin. It still draws its devotees; [if perhaps only to take the waters for their curative properties.] There are two 'pools' located within the church grounds one of which is dedicated to the founder saint the other to Saint Catherine. (This information comes from the pamphlet *Guide to Saint Doulagh's* which issued in 2000 following the restoration of the church in 1990 — and the rehabilitation of Saint Catherine's 'pond' in 1969.) The name of the church's dedicatory saint seems to be of Hiberno-Norse, the language in use in Fingal at the time of the arrival of the Grace Dieu canonesses to the area.[66] Its form is typically 'Do-Olaf 'a reminiscence of Saint Olaf, the great Scandinavian saint[66/67] The founders seem nevertheless to have been Augustinian (Aroassian) nuns from Clonard and not the Grace Dieu canonesses who succeeded them. These nuns must have been in possession of earlier traditions of the area from before the arrival of the canonesses.

---

[66] **Dr. William Reeves,** the noted nineteenth century antiquary disputed that 'the Church of' 'St Diulach' was called after the Norse saint (Dublin NLI Call No. Ir 726). In Wexford it seems to have taken the Hiberno- Norse form. According to **Edward Culleton** (1999). **Father Gwynn** refers to a place 'Kealdulex' in the Lands of Sitric, King of Dublin at the time of the Battle of Clontarf. Sitric's father was Olaf Cuaran the Christian King of Dublin who abdicated in order to end his days in Iona. No authority known to this present writer admits that the church is named after the saintly Olaf Cuaran but it seems that it may well be.

[67] *Several Decretal Letters from* Rome mention 'Trian Clothair' church which is also thought to be an early name of Saint Doulagh's. Prof. **Otway Ruthven** doubts if it was amongst the see-lands of the archbishop of Dublin. See her *Church Lands of County Dublin* in *Medieval Studies* (Dublin 1961 p.60). Yet Archbishop Cumin, purported to grant lands under that description to Christ Church. Saint Doulagh's is also taxed under the same name in the Papal Taxation of 1291 The name suggests it may have been an outlier in possession of the diocese of Clogher at that time (See paragraph 'Interlude 2' above.) It seems more than probable that the Clonard nuns *were* aware of Saint Catherine. A very good sketch of St. Doulagh's where the well appears is to be found at p.299 of **John Savages** *Picturesque Ireland* (New York 1884) See photograph on P108 herein.

Figure No. 12. Holy Well at Fieldstown, Fingal, County Dublin

Figure No. 15. Sketch of remains of ruined nursery of **Grace Dieu**,
Canonesses at Lusk by Brendan Scally

(Margaret Gowan's report on Grace Dieu, Townland site and lands is mentioned in
Isabel Bennet's (Ed) *Excavations 1988* (Dublin 1989) which refers to 65 burials
excavated during the course of the gas pipeline work through the townland).

Griffith's Park, Drumcondra, Holy Well

Of the several other Holy Wells remarked upon by **O Danachair** in County Dublin and dedicated to Saint Catherine he nearly missed an important one, only mentioning it in a later issue of *Reportorium Novum*. That is Griffith Park Holy Well, Dublin.

The Grace Dieu canonesses had property in Drumcondra and it seems likely that this Holy Well is located in what was their former lands there of Clonliffe—part of which is now Griffith Park. It is a relatively unknown Holy Well though located in what is a central area of the City. It did not appear on the Ordnance Maps until late in the nineteenth century when it was also inserted in the maps of **Alex Thom's** *Directory*. Its location - or rather where it used to be - may now only be found by searching for the brass plaque affixed to railings of the Park (near Drumcondra Library).

It, is described in an article by Father o'Leary entitled "Saint Catherine's Holy Well, Drumcondra, County Dublin" published in JRSAI for December 1928. In it he shows in illustration a pleasant niche structure (described as 'a rude pointed arch'). Since then, this has been demolished along with the 'Holy Well' itself, the 'spout' which was diverted by the Corporation Parks Department and replaced by a shrubbery. 'The spout', a sort of culvert of the time, piped the water across the road from a garden in Melbourne Avenue (now a derelict site, once built over where the original Well had been) The water now disappears, evidently into a drain discharging to the River Tolka.[68]

---

[68] A worthwhile heritage project for the present City Council to carry out might be to rehabilitate the original Holy Well in the Melbourne Avenue site if the public did not have access to it for water to drink.

CHAPTER 9

The Cult of Saint Catherine in the dioceses of Cork and Cloyne[69]

Cork city and the shoreline of its harbour was an area of considerable settlement for Vikings and their descendants, the Ostmen. It was re-settled by the Anglo-Normans in the early thirteenth century. They took a firm hold over the lands of the native Irish (and the Ostmen) throughout a large area. Their ecclesiastics duly followed but one must assume they were preceded by clerics speaking the Hiberno-Norse patois.

Again, many of these Anglo-Norman clergy came (based on what has been shown earlier) from the Somerset-Gloucestershire area. It is also probable that not a few came from France and were fully Norman. It may be noted that the Benedictine 'priories' (they were but 'cells' in point of fact) in Waterford, and that of Saint John the Evangelist in Cork, were endowed by Saint Peter's, Bath. They were founded in ca.1192. under Prince John and were to act as hospitals. They were shortly absorbed by the Hospitallers of Kilmainham., Dublin. The church of Saint John however continued as a parish church for Cork. (Located near the South Gate, this church had a chantry altar dedicated to Saint Catherine which is referred to in the Will of John Wychendon (1306). In this Will there were provisions made for its upkeep.)

The arrival of the Victorines to Cork in the closing years of the twelfth century also seems to have been instituted by Saint Thomas's Abbey, Dublin, surprisingly not Saint Catherine's Abbey, Waterford. The Cork church ('Saint Catherine's') was thereafter affiliated with St Thomas's. The congregation was later combined with the community of Shandon to form the 'parish of Saint Catherine'. The aforementioned Wychendon Will also contains bequests "to the canons of Saint Victor of the church of Saint Catherine" This church was to remain parochial up to 1523 when it became appropriate to the Cistercian abbey of Chore, Midleton County Cork.[70]

---

[69] The information contained in these paragraphs is largely taken from Rev **Sr. Evelyn Bolster's** *A History of the Diocese of Cork Part* I (Shannon 1972)

[70]**See Patrick O'Flanagan and Cornelius G. Buttimer** (Eds.) their *Cork History and Society* (Dublin 1993) p.9

Ballynoe

Dr **A.F. O'Brien** in his paper *Cork and South East Region ca.1170 to 1583.*[71] shows how the growth of active market towns was so important for the local economy at the time. He mentions, among several such centres, Ballynoe in east Cork.[72] This is to-day a village having ruins of a medieval church dedicated to Saint Catherine of Alexandria. Ballynoe is in fact only one of six Irish parishes which now bear a surviving cultic reminiscence of Saint Catherine by virtue of her Feast Day being still celebrated with religious ceremony in the churches of the parish. Unusually, she is patron of each of the three churches of Conna-Ballynoe Parish, (though at Conna Saint Catherine is jointly with Saint Columba)

Located today in the diocese of Cloyne, Ballvnoe forms just one part of the Roman Catholic parish. The Cistercian monastery at Middleton (referred to as 'Chore Benediciti' in documents) had lands in the twelfth and thirteenth centuries in the east of Cork County - in the Anglo-Norman Deanery of Ocurblethan. It is possible that some of the older monks were former canons who had moved from Saint Catherine's, Cork, to join the Cistercians (when the former church and parish ceased to function) If they retained devotion to their saint within their new community it would not be surprising if they took the opportunity of giving her name to the modest outlying church at Ballynoe, the ruins of which may be discerned to-day.

(This part of East Cork was well settled by the Anglo-Norman colonists from the earliest days: Youghal and Lismore were strong centres of their power. Despite its present modest size "Newtown Ballynoe" was for a time an important centre of the Barry family in their lands of 'Ocurblethan'. The area formed part of the nominal Earldom of Desmond and in due course formed part of the Barony of Kinataloon) The Signature of the Abbot of Saint Catherine's Abbey, Waterford, is appended to the surviving Black Book of the Cathedral of Cloyne of the Fourteenth century.[73]

---

[71] **A.F.O'Brien** *The Cork and South Coast (1170-to 1583) Part VI pp 140-*147 in **O'Flanagan and Buttimer** (1993). (It appears to be a candidate for speculating pre Anglo- Norman settlement direct from Normandy)

[72] In *Dinnseanchas (Nollaig 1965)*, **Liam O Buachalla** *asserts* that "Kilconnan" was an early form of the name of Ballynoe. This could mean that it was contained within the lands of the Cistercian abbey of De Castro Dei, (Fermoy),·and not therefore related at all to the abbey of Chore, Middleton,as suggested in the text above. Kilconnan, in **O Buachalla's** document, may however be a reference, to Conna and not to Ballynoe. From. another early document (1391),it appears `Nyeton' was on the bounds of Ocurblethan- ('Olethan') and perhaps in a separate Deanery from Conna. See *Dirmseanchas* (Nollaig *1966) p. 45*. Of course, it may be no mere coincidence that the feast day of St. Colman Mac Lenin, the Patron Saint of the Diocese of Cloyne, falls on 24th November.

[73] Alternatively **MacCotter** (KAHS IV 2004) says that Elias Fitz Norman contributed to many ecclesiastical benefices of Saint Catherine's Abbey, Waterford, which were located in Co Cork in the ear;y twelfth century. Ballynoe may have been one of them, quite independent possibly of any Cistercian connection

He and the bishop of the diocese of Cloyne, where Ballynoe was due to be included, had a special interest in the matter when the adjoining Lismore Diocese was about to be wound up. The portion which included the parish of Conna-Ballynoe was to be detached from Lismore diocese and added to the Diocese of Cloyne. There is a record in the ancient "Annals of Youghal" for 1347 of a priest being presented from some important English centre -"to the Church of Saint Catherine of Neweton which is within the gift of the Crown" (described thus in the royal mandate).

Youghal was a town having a considerable population of Somerset people settled there. "Neweton" is the English form of Ballynoe (Baile Nua " the New Town"). This form would have been that used by an English royal scrivener preparing the mandate.[74]

The Diocese of Lismore ceased to exist as an independent entity in 1363, becoming joined to Waterford Diocese. Its breaking up involved a redistribution of territory; no doubt receiving the attention of the aforementioned priest who had been presented to Ballynoe. A large part of the Deanery of Ocurblethan went to the diocese of Cloyne in the settlement of affairs

Gwynn and Hadcock suggest alternatively that the mediaeval church ruin at Ballynoe may have been a foundation of the Knights Hospitallers. If so it could have been by way of being a branch of their house at Rincrew eight miles away. The Hospitallers were, however not particularly renowned for being patrons of Saint Catherine. A mile from Rincrew, however, in the townland of Rearour, is a Holy Well called 'Tobar a' Chailin' (named as such in 1940.) Its site is on the bounds of the parish of Conna-Ballynoe and the ancient parish of 'Ryncro'[75] Its name may be a folk distortion of 'Tobar Chaitlín", otherwise "Catherine's Holy Well" and not simply 'The Girl's well' as traditionally understood.

---

[74] *Information* from Pamphlet, *The Parish of Ballynoe* (Middleton 2000). See also **Denis Power's** *Archaeological Inventory of Co. Cork Vol. 2 (East and South* Cork, par. 5613) (Dublin 1994). According to RV (615)(Cloyne) Ballynoe was a vicarage supplied by the College of Youghal in the fourteenth century. The priest supplied in 1347was "Richard Cristian, Clerk" who may have been a papal assignment

[75] See **P.J.Hartnett** The *Holy Wells of East Muskerry* in *Béaloidas'*(1940). The supposed distortion of the name of the Holy Well at Rearour is parallelled at Rush, County Dublin(Fingal) where **O Donachair** notes a Well he calls 'Tobar a' Chailín'. At Rush, a nearby housing estate there is aptly called 'Saint Catherine's Park'. But here there is also a Holy Well known for 'Saint Catherine'

But even if there is some uncertainty as to the cultic origin of their parish's name, the people of Ballynoe still hold Saint Catherine of Alexandria in high regard. Many social activities are called after Saint Catherine and the parishioners are very proud to have such a special patron. The Roman Catholic Church there has a fine stained glass window depicting the saint in standard pose. (See Figure 13) There is a similar window for St. Columba in the Church at nearby Conna. At Cobh R.C. Cathedral there are other windows representing the patron saints of each of the parishes of the diocese of Cloyne.)[76]

Figure No. 13 Stained glass window in the church
of Saint Catherine of Alexandria at Ballynoe, County Cork

---

[76] Illustrations and information provided by Padraigh Mac Amhlaoibh.of Cóbh Kind permission has also been granted for the Ballynoe window's reproduction by the publishers of the pamphlet. (See Figure 11)

CHAPTER 10

The Cult of Saint Catherine in the R.C. dioceses of Kerry and Limerick.
The United C.O.I. diocese of Limerick, Aghadoe and Ardfert.

North Kerry and the Dingle peninsula were also quite heavily colonised by the
Anglo-Normans from early in the thirteenth century. As already outlined, the Anglo-
Irish Church entered enthusiastically into a full reorganisation of parishes under the
administration of bishops adapting to English ways with the full support of
the popes of the time.[77] The southern coast of the Dingle peninsula, which the
incomers referred to as 'Osurreys', (otherwise Irish Aos Iorruis, a name with Viking
connotations.) While displacing part of the ancient name which they corruptly
applied to a new large territory called 'Corcaguiny' the area formerly known as
Corca Dhuibhne is used again to-day for the ancient district comprising most of the
Dingle Peninsula.

The peninsula was important because of its convenient harbours (notably Dingle)
and for its trade with England and France for many generations Vessels from Rouen
and other distant shores were engaged in export of fish and importation of wines.
Later in the period, during the rebellions of the fifteenth/sixteenth centuries,
Edmund Curtis in his *Medieval History* notes that Dingle was one of the few
English boroughs of Munster to remain loyal to the crown.[78] Early accounts further
support the existence of a considerable colony of English settlers around the then
villages of ('Dingleycuish') Dingle and ('Bantry') Ventry for a long time.

Miss **M.A.Hickson**, the noted Kerry antiquary, points out[79] that in the Papal
Taxation of 1300 Aghadoe is listed as a Deanery dedicated to Saint Catherine.
Aghadoe is now a village a few miles west of Killarney but in the fourteenth
century as a Deanery comprised a diocese covering a very wide area (though at the
same time not encompassing Osurreys which was in Ardfert Diocese/Deanery.
These deaneries latter was incorporated much later into the R.C.Diocese of Kerry)

---

[77] See **Paul Mac Cotter's** *Lordship and Colony in Anglo-Norman Kerry* (1177-1600) in Journal of the Kerry Archaeological and Historical Society (2004)

[78] See **M.A.Hickson's** *Selections from old Kerry Records* (London 1872 and 1874) See also her *Notes on Kerry Topography* in JRSAI (1889) p. 116

[79] *(Baile Atha Cliath 1939)* See his *Triocadh-céad Chorca Dhuíbhne Cuid* 1 in *Béaloideas (Baile Atha Cliath 1937) ll.57 &rl*

It is recorded that in the thirteenth century Saint Catherine's Abbey, Waterford, had several appropriate rectories in the Deanery of Aghadoe from which they drew rents. With the decay of Waterford Abbey in the fourteenth/fifteenth centuries, the right to these rents, continued, and were taken up by the lay landowners who succeeded. According to **MacCotter**, the see of Ardfert also had many such rents in large areas of Osurreys Deanery near Dingle. The inference is that knowledge of Saint Catherine and her name was propagated during their collection whether by clergy or lay. (In Chapter 15 is put forward another way knowledge of Saint Catherine might have came to the Dingle peninsula. It comes from a suggestion made on general principles whereby such tales may be received, occuring in the historian **Kathleen Hughes**' book *Early Christian Ireland* (N.Y. 1972) p.166)

Ventry church (that is, Ceann Tra.) is to-day in the enlarged parish of Dingle and is dedicated to Naomh Caitlin, otherwise 'Naomh Caitriona' that is Saint Catherine of Alexandria as is clear from the 25th of November being the day her Feast is celebrated Some aspects of the pattern have been documented by **Padraig O Siochfradha, ('An Seabhac')**.[80] Another Irish language writer, **Peig Sayers**, in her autobiography *Macthnamh Seana-mhna*. tells of her attendance at 'Naomh Caitlín's pattern in the 1920's, detailing the activities, prayers recited etc.[81]

At Ventry, the folklore purports to provide an account of Naomh Caitlin's relics being washed ashore at Ceann Tra 'in a barrel' after having been floated off on a naobhog by the King of Rome.[81] The tale survives here in a much more degenerate form than the equivalent which circulated in Killybegs. The colony of Ventry, (the members of which by the fourteenth century were English)[82], may have suffered by the mid sixteenth century a degree of isolation from the home country and the Pale.

---

[80] Kind informant Micheál O Dubhláin O.S. (RIP He died in May 2006). An Gráig, Baile an Fheirtéirigh. In *Bealoideas* 1959 Iml 27.p.73 is an additional account to that of **P.O. Siochru** of the rites practised at Ventry. In the Irish Language, it was taken down by the folklore collector **Sean O Dubhda**. At the time there was a clear recollection amongst those frequenting the two-day celebration of Naomh Caitriona's "turas", of there having once been a ruined building in the burial ground attached to the chapel which the procession circled around. A special Indulgence could be gained by those participating in the rituals of the Feast-day. Cures were expected for head-pains. It was said that a Vision of the saint used once be seen by early risers on Saint Catherine's Day but this ceased when proselytising settlers arrived and one was buried in the cemetery.

[81] An early *Life of Saint Catherine* in the Old Czech Language, which circulated in the area of Bohemia / Moravia corresponding to present day Slovenia, states a Holy Roman Emperor won a battle on 25th November. It has recently been translated into English by **Thomas Head** and appears in his *Medieval Hagiography (London 2000)*

[82] Until the battle of Callan(-afersey) 1261, the Anglo-Normans had been pouring in to Osurreys. the two principal towns of which were Killorglin and Dingle. Godfrey de Mareis on a King John grant was the main leader, developing his colonising on the back of the several churches he founded. At his death he settled his patrimony on his cousin Emmaline de Longspee's on her husband, Maurice Fitz Maurice and on several minor relations. But extensive litigation ensued between them. Emmaline, however outlasted all the claiments. Under subsequent inter family relationships as described by **MacCotter** *The Earls of Desmond* and their agnatic offspring (The Knights of Kerry) retained their hold on Osurreys, sufficient for the purposes of this account to note that the stronghold at CeannTrá (at Rahinane) was theirs until the sixteenth century. See also **Saml Lewis Dictionary** (1837)'Dingle' for later still.

By the seventeenth the purity of their stock may have declined to such an extent as to be unable to hand down traditions intact. (In Chapter 17 below will be learned some reasons why this may be better understood). The resultant population, loyal to Dublin, retained only a distorted version off Saint Catherine's Life and cult. On the other hand in Killybegs, clerical preservation of the cult benefited by a manuscript Life that had been in circulation there from the sixteenth century. (Again see below Chapter 13 for details)

An interesting village 'twinning' relationship has recently been sponsored at Ventry (through a Televis na Gaeilge, TG4 programme) with the village of Landava in Slovenia. Both share Saint Katherine as their patron and they both honour the saint on the 25th November. (The Landava tradition alleging that monks brought the cult from Ireland is mentioned in the TG4 Programme. It is not, however, well merited). At Ventry the annual penitential rounds take place in the churchyard, presumably where the saintly remains of an unknown devotee from the sea are interred.

Figure No. 14 A tapestry showing Naomh Caitríona in typical pose (prepared locally, it hangs in Sáipéal Naomh Chaitríona, Ceann Trá, Dingle, Co. Kerry

Saint Catherine's Point, Allihies, Co. Cork

This is a modern misnomer for the headland, perhaps alluding to the name of the southernmost headland of the Isle of Wight. The sight of the latter is often assumed to have been greeted with relief by navigators of ships coming up the Channel after a long voyage. They would had been praying to Saint Catherine that their sightings and calculations had been correct.

The proper name for the point of land in Allihies. County Cork, is,however, 'Kilcatherine Point'. One can see how easily the change has come about, possibly through a colloquial usage of the Cable Telegraph's staff from nearby Valencia Island. (Many of whom may themselves have come from the Isle of Wight, as travelling directly by sea, was the most convenient manner of staffing the station.) The church site of Kilcatherine and parish of the same name does indeed resonate of Saint Catherine as if her cult were well known in the locality. In point of fact, during the thirteenth century Saint Catherine's Abbey, Waterford were in possession of the church of Kilmocomoge, Barony of Carbery, County Cork.[83] This was the principal church for Bantry Bay and Beara according to **Bolster**(1972). The parish of Kilcatherine came within its ambit although it was in the diocese of Kerry. The spelling in a papal Decretal Letter of 1199 is Cellchatthigern after the local saint, Naomh Cathtighern.[84]

Chapter 11 **Limerick and Kerry Diocese** (Continued) on page *78*

---

[83] See **Maurice P. Sheehy** (Dublin 1962)p.143 also **Evelyn Bolster** (Shannon 1972) *p.87, and* **Newport B. White** *(Dublin 1943)* p346. For another reference to Kilcatherine parish, see **Micheal Mac Carthaigh** in *Dinnseanchas* (Dublin, Meitheamh 1972)

[84] *Pontificia Hibernica* I p 108 1962

INTERLUDE NO. 2

The Victorine canons (3.)

The diocese of Down and Connor in the fifteenth century

We know little about Thomas, the first bishop of Down and Connor who was introduced from Saint Catherine's Abbey, Waterford to Downpatrick, but quite a lot about his successor, Thady. (the 'Thadeus' of the Latin of the documents). He also was translated from Waterford where he too had been Abbot Thady became bishop from 1469 to 1486.[85] His surname was Ombrissa, probably a corrupt form of O Muirghiosa anglicised Morrissey. He began his career as a canon regular of Saint Augustine at Saint Catherine's Abbey. Waterford. There he, a native Irishman, must have displayed exceptional talent and impressed his superiors with his ability for adapting to the English protocols for the reform of the Irish church, (that is, for its Romanisation[86] from being formerly Celtic)

Thady received his first promotion when sent as prior to the monastery of Mothel about twelve miles from Waterford. Mothel was an Aroassian re- foundation of the early thirteenth century under the patronage of the former Saints Cuan and Brogan of Ballynevin. The Celtic monks had settled at Ballynevin but moved to Mothel after a plague. (**Gwynn and Hadcock** suggest 1204). It is not known when they adopted the Augustinian Rule but under it they created the priory of Mothel. It lies near the village of Clonea (Power), County Waterford. The visitor to the site may clearly detect the stages of its development from the rather rudimentary beginnings left by the monks of Cuan. The beginnings of Mothel, however, were not propitious as, probably after another plague (fourteenth century - the Black Death, the Aroassian community became greatly depleted. The Victorine canons from Waterford were called upon to take over and Thady became the new prior. They were evidently successful and erected the substantial Priory, the fine ruins of which may be seen to-day.[87]

[85] See **Dr. William Reeves'** *Ecclesiastical History of the Diocese of Down and Connor (Dublin 1847)* Thomas of Waterford (1445-1468) is not, however recognised in *the New History of Ireland* (1982), Succession Lists for the Dioceses. See also **Aubrey Gwynn's** *Medieval Armagh* (Dundalk 1946) p.136/137 for his successor - "Thadeus".For him The Statutes of Kilkenny passed in 1367 against any Irish being appointed bishop in an English Church apparently did not apply !
NOTE Thadeus was granted The 'Augustinian' Saint Mary's Priory, Kells in commendam at his appointment as bishop. It may be concluded this Priory was Victorine. Also if canons had acquired the adjoining Columban abbey in the thirteenth century, as some say, St. Mary's probably could well afford to give bishop Thadeus a share of their tithes in the fifteenth. Another matter of some interest that it raises is the possibility of the Victorines of Kells introducing Saint Catherine to the parish of Oristown, hardly four miles away, for which see Chapter 17

[86] See Chapter entitled *An English Culture?* pp..18ff in **Nigel Saul** (Ed) *The Oxford Illustrated History of Medieval England* (Oxford 1997)

[87] See article by ' M.M.' *The Abbey of Mothel, Co Waterford* in *North Munster Antiquarian Journal (1959)* and **Canon Power's** pamphlet *The Story of Mothel* (Published by the National Graves Association (nd. *ca.1930.)*

Whatever the Victorines' relationship with the Dominicans of the Black Abbey, Kilkenny may have been, it is unknown today, but perhaps it was the well known satisfactory submission at the time of both to secular authority. Mothel Priory was able to make over to the friars, two fifths of their tithes from 1437. The friars probably received their statue of Saint Catherine from the canons about that time too. (This statue, reputedly of the fourteenth century, was only discovered in 1825 under plasterwork in the friary. See Figure No. 3). Thady had been sent out to Mothel as prior ca. 1444 (perhaps to oversee this extraordinary provision as well as to become the refounder)

Thady coped well with his extra burdens since, after some years, (in about 1455) he was then sent on to Molana Abbey, County Waterford, another abbey similarly placed (That is to say, it had been Aroassian from being previously Celtic.). Thady's new monastery was already an important onethough maintaining a strong Celtic ethos in the Céilí Dé tradition. (It had been renowned for learning under the name of 'Dair Inis'. One suspects he was sent there on a mission of Romanisation. There is evidence that when he left there the number of canons was greatly increased there)

Molana abbey was located on what is almost an island near the mouth of the river Blackwater near Youghal. (The present ruins are substantial) [88] Thady appears not to have been able to make much progress on this assignment initially probably from resistance from the Céilí Dé, but, as a thoroughly experienced churchman, he was called to become prior/abbot of his home abbey of Saint Catherine's Waterford ca.1462. (The date 1473, given in **Gwynn and Hadcock** seems incorrect, otherwise this account of Thady's career is largely taken from it.)

We do not know if Saint Catherine's cult ever took root at Molana; There is no evidence for it nor should it be expected. The monastery, of course, was within the periphery of Rincrew, Ballynoe, Youghal, Lismore, and Cork, where there was devotion to the saint. Thady's undoubted personal commitment to the patron of his congregation must also have been a factor. Yet it is entirely credible that at Molana, where Celtic religion had been paramount until recently, it is very unlikely that the cause of Saint Catherine would make progress . (Thady may have attended services in her honour at the Kinsalebeg grange which was Benedictine and only three miles away). Mothel, on the other hand, by way of confirming its allegiance to the saint's

---

[88] See **Canon Power's** article *The Abbey of Molana* (JRSAI 1932 Pt. II). The Superior of this abbey granted the revenues of Saint Mochua's church at Darragh in County Limerick to the Bishop of Limerick in 1267. The latter site is not mentioned by **Gwynn and Hadcock** but a link with Keynsham may be suspected. **Canon Power** supplies no information on whether any of the canons *at* Molana might have been Victorines, though he was familiar with them at Waterford.

cult, has one piece of effigeal sculpture of Saint Catherine from the late fifteenth century on a tomb there and also, of course, the priory had given their effigy of the saint to Kilkenny.[89]

Thady was prior/abbot at Saint Catherine's Waterford only seven years when he was called to Down and Connor (and informally Dromore[90]) as Bishop in 1469. He was consecrated at Rome in the church of Minerva. (Power after Ware). His reputation as an effective ecclesiastic must have preceded him. It is stated (Power) that he caused much of the revenue of Saint Catherine's Abbey to be united to the see of Down and Connor resulting in its great decline.[91]

At Downpatrick his devotion to Saint Catherine must also have been evident. The much revered wooden statue of the saint held at the cathedral, is mentioned in the Annals of Ulster in 1538 on the occasion of its being -"carried off by the Saxons" (that is, during the Henrician Dissolution). This may be taken as evidence of the continuation after his death of bishop Thady's veneration for the saint. In the Church of Ireland diocese of Connor to this day the parish of Killead (Crumlin) is dedicated to Saint Catherine. This also suggests that a tradition existed there going back to the two bishops from Waterford who came to the diocese in the fifteenth century.

When Bishop Thady came to his Diocese of Down and Connor he found much as had experienced at Waterford, the celtic sites struggling perhaps with Ceili De efforts towards improvement of observance. At Muckamore was one of the larger such monastic sites in Connor. Thady apparently determined to introduce the Augustinian Rite but unusually, since the Arossians were the established group at nearly Armagh, he introduced Victorians probably from his old St. Catheine's Priory at Waterford. It may be inferred from **Gwynn and Hancock's** account (p.188) that he may have actually displaced earlier Aroassians there.

[89] See pamphlet by Rev **Hugh Fenning** O.P. (Kilkenny nd ca.1996) pp 12-13 and 54, also **John Hunt** (1974) According to **MacNeill** (Lughnasa 1965-82) St.Cuan, the patron of Aghascragh was a substitute for the tutelary god of the harvest.The C.O.I. church at Aghascragh is dedicated to Saint Catherine. Saint Mary's Holy Well at Mothel is stated to have been dedicated to Saints Cuan and Brogan in times past. The pattern at Mothel (mid July) is clearly for Lughnasa though not listed by **MacNeill**. The substitution of the Virgin Mother instead of the Virgin Martyr as the dedicatrix of the Holy Well there is a not really surprising.

[90] The (English) Archbishops of Armagh had great difficulty in attracting Englishmen consecrated for the diocese of Dromore to come and officiate. (See **Fr Michael Robson** O.F.M.writing on *Nicholas Warter. Franciscan Bishop of Dromore (1372-1448)* in *Collectanea Hibernica* (Naas 2000) p.8)

[91] Thomas Fitzgerald, Lord of Decies (whose seat was Dungarvan Castle) retained the First Fruits of the new Rector of the church of St. Mary, Dungarvan (Henry Burnham) 1440 stating that they were not due since Dungarvan's church was united to the Abbey of Keynsham through its connection with the Farm at Abbeyside (**Power's** *'Annates Waterfordensis* (**Archivium Hibernicum** 1946) (See the Aerial Survey on p 115.) The matter was referred to Rome by the Bishop of Lismore. The pope (Martyn V) declared that Keynsham Abbey had no such rights over Dungarvan, The First Fruits were to be passed to the Holy Office, and St. Catherine' Abbey Waterford was ordered to be fined 50 golden sovereigns. In the Calebdar of Papal Registers, Letters p.352 it is stated 1448 that as a result of the large part of the revenues of St. Catherines Priory Waterford going to Diocee of Down and Conner "Divine worship is diminished, hospitality not kept and the substance of the Priory desippated"

CHAPTER 11

Limerick and Kerry Diocese (Continued)

Black Nuns of O'Conyl (Connello Barony) Co. Limerick

Much mystery formerly surrounded the whereabouts of the head-house of 'the Black Nuns of O'Conyl '(which was simply known to be in the Barony of "Connello") It was not until **John Wardell** published his article on the subject in 1904[92] that its identity was satisfactorily explained. The problem was caused by several other places being called "Na Cailleacha Dubha" (The Black Nuns) claiming the honour. The habit they wore as Augustinian canonesses distinguished them probably from other nuns of the time who wore white following the native Irish practise. Much of this **Wardell** was able to elucidate, consequently excluding these various other sites. He was able to focus his attention on the ruins at Old Abbey House, lying between Shanagolden and Foynes in the Parish of Robertstown.

He concluded from the relatively extensive nature of the ruins that he had discovered the main centre. **Dianne Hall** has since updated **Wardell** in her book[93] and reproduced illustrations of the western door and an effigy in the piscina. The latter is interesting as it displays a 'nun' pointing to an amulet worn around her neck depicting a wheel(see figure 3 p 13). It appears to be of Saint Catherine. Dr.William Reeves the noted ecclesiastical historian and bishop of Down, Connor and Dromore knew of Monasternagalliagh as 'Saint. Catherine's' as a result of its being mentioned in the Elizabethan Fiants with which he was familiar. The queen granted the "monastery and its appurtenances" to Warram St Leger in 1578. shortly after the rebellion of the earl of Desmond had been put down by Sir Richard Maltby in 1574.(According to Inquisitions of Chief Remembrancer, the "former Abbey of Nenughle of Saint Catherine" was later taken from Maltby 'the rent not being paid).[94]

The earliest documentary mention of the convent describes it "as in the possession of one Thomas FitzMaurice in 1298 his grandfather having granted certain lands to the nuns".[95]

---

[92] It appears in JRSAI *The History and Antiquities of Saint Catherine's Old Abbey County Limerick*
[93] *Women in the Church in Medieval Ireland* (Dublin 2003) p.106-7
[94] IRC Mss (Dublin, 1991)
[95] At the same time it is mentioned in the Papal Taxation of 1291 when it was styled "the house of Saint Katherine in O'Conyl"

Waterford

The Victorines having been so much involved in the history of the cult of Saint Catherine in Ireland already, it will not surprise the reader that Saint Catherine's abbey at Waterford was also prominent here. **T.J. Westropp** noted [96] that a number of Limerick churches [including Askeaton and Ballingarry] had been granted to Keynsham Abbey and that the bishop of Limerick had, in 1237, "procured their restitution from a canon of Keynsham.' (We know his name from other sources as John de Bineford)

The Abbey of Saint Catherine at Waterford is also recorded as having been awarded the rectorship of a church at Askeaton in the same year, (accomplished by the same canon?). Askeaton is only a few miles from Saint. Catherine's. Moreover **Waddell** refers to the dissolution of the convent in 1574 when Queen Elizabeth's new Commissioners found that Henry VIII's former Commissioners "had been duped". (The nuns had seemingly 'concealed the rectories of New Grange and Dunmoylyn (Darragh?) and also "the presentation of the Vicarages"). It transpires that the church at Askeaton had been long under the control of Keynsham Abbey, the abbey evidently administering it all along until the final Suppression in 1603.

---

[96] In his article *Askeaton, County Limerick* in JRSAI (1903) p. 29 and ff, but see also Proceedings of Somerset Archaeological and Natural History Society Vol. 53 (1907)

Figure No. 16 Figure Sculpture of Saint Catherine at St. Mary's Church (C.O.I.)
Callan, Co. Kilkenny (from **Hunt's** *Irish medieval figure Sculpture* Vol II,
Cat. No. 94 p.321

CHAPTER 12

Anglo-Norman / English custom for the churches of diocese of Meath

Anglo-norman ecclesiastics in the thirteenth century, with the backing of the newly arrived great colonial lords, founded many abbeys and nunneries in the Pale. Much church lands, vacated by the Irish, were taken over by the newly religious houses. The larger Dublin abbeys and priories sent out monks to "granges". (That is farms held for the home abbots which were mainly engaged in the supply of produce for them; these, again, were often abandoned native monastic settlements).The Abbey of St. Thomas' and the priory of the Knights Hospitallers of Kilmainham, both in Dublin, were houses which had several granges in County Meath and also in Counties Cork, Tipperary and Limerick.

The Augustinian Priory, Newtown-Trim.

By the end of the thirteenth century Trim, in the County Meath, acted as a sort of beachhead-town within a wedge of the Pale and was designed as a bulwark against the "wild" or native Irish, most notably the lords of Breffni. This was standard strategy for the Anglo-Normans, who also built up security in the form of groups of strong castles, in combinations with what appear to be fortified churches.

The Victorines had an early (**MacCotter** says 1202) priory at Newtown-Trim situated below the main town of Trim on the north bank of the River Boyne in close proximity to an imposing ruined structure, the former Cathedral[97] There was also a strong house of Crutch Friars on the south bank. All three structures practically ran together for defensive purposes. A second Victorine priory, albeit smaller, seems to have existed at Kells utilising the defences of the old Columban monastery for protection. (At the time in question the Columban monks had retreated to Derry in the face of Anglo-Norman pressures) It must be said that neither of these Victorine priories of Kells and Newtown - Trim provide direct evidence of an attachment to Saint Catherine. (Victorine Canons from Kells may arguably have been responsible for the dedication of a hill-top church at Oristown to her in the thirteenth century but see below, next section, for an alternative theory)

---

[97] **Noel E.French** (n.d.) in his *Trim.Places and Traces* has a panoramic view at p.50.

The many pilgrims to Trim stood in awe of a famous wooden effigy of the Blessed Virgin held by the Aroassian priory of Saint Mary's in the town. (The Yellow Steeple stands on the site. The Priory burned down in 1396 but was replaced elsewhere).

The Victorines dedicated their priory just three miles away also to Saint Mary. It is probable that at such an early date many of the early Victorine canons at Newtown-Trim came directly from France, some from Keynsham in Somerset. The abbey at Keynsham was also dedicated to Saint Mary. Their lack of fervour for Saint Catherine's cult says much about its decline amongst the canons since the death of King Henry. According to **Hennessy** there was a Guild of Saint Catherine in the Parish Church of Trim later[98].

The canons who went to Bridgetown from Newtown-Trim when it was first founded (ca.1207) also dedicated it to Saint Mary. Intercession of Saint Catherine then would have been through private prayers only, if at all.

Saint Catherine's Church at Telltown/Oristown.

At Telltown (the mythological Tailltean) about four miles from Kells there is a ruined medieval church which was curiously dedicated to Saint Catherine of Alexandria. It is located close to the modern Telltown House at Oristown in an old burial ground within an enclosure which archaeologists think may be pre-Christian. It is on a hill-top fairly central to the sacred area whereon the Assembly or Feis of Aonach Tailtean used to take place annually about the pagan sacred time of Lughnasa (the first day of August or within a week either side of that date[99]). This festival, or Feis ("Wedding feast") held such a powerful attraction for the people of Ireland that it straddled the introduction of Christianity. As it also formed part of the annual inaugural rites of the Árd-Rí or central High King of nearby Tara it was practically impossible to eradicate, certainly in the Midlands. The Feis met more or less annually until the eleventh century and "survived in an attenuated form until the nineteenth century."[100]

---

[98] See **RIA** *Irish Historic Towns Atlas No 14.* (Dublin 2004). The Parish Church in question no longer exists and may have been housed in the former Priory of Canons Regular of St. Augustine. Could not some of the Canons have passed on the devotion to the Saint to those who followed on within a parish structure?

[99] See **Maire MacNeill's** *The Festival of Lughnasa* (Oxford 1962, reprinted with additions 1982) pp 315 ff and 318ff. The mythological background, (pp 320—324) provided by her is convenient. She does consider the matter of the presence of the Medieval church of Saint Catherine near Teltown House. but does not elaborate. The consensus of scholars is that Armagh clerical intervention resulted in a reconversion of Donaghpatrick in the ninth century.

[100] See Prof. **Francis, John Byrne's** *Irish Kings and High Kings* (London 1973) p.31

Until christianised in ca.800, the Assembly perpetuated the claim of the High King in the ancient belief that he and his ancestors were earthlings bound to Great Mother Earth as if by marriage. Any denial of these tenets was believed to provoke malevolent spirits who could harm the immediate harvest or be hostile to other activities of the year until the next Lughnasa Festival (in England 'Lammas') came around. The antiquarian **John O'Donovan**, when submitting his observations to the Ordnance Survey Office during his travels throughout County Meath between 1832 and 1838, determined from ancient documents that the centre of the Aonach was not the rath or burial ground in which the old church ruin lay but another, a more imposing, triple rampart ring fort near Donaghpatrick called Ros Airthir, 'the Western Grove.'[101]

If we accept that the National Patron travelled there in the fifth century, (and this is disputed but also rationalised as meaning 'Patricians' from Armagh) it was Donaghpatrick where Saint Patrick focused his evangelising efforts and with some success. It has not really been explained by modern scholars why the Tripartite Life of Saint Patrick which relates these events, ignored the importance of the ancient Burial Ground on Teltown Hill the 'Sacral' site of the area. **Catherine Swift** in a recent article,[103] however directs attention to it and concludes that the aura of the site (in Irish language blai an aonaigh) was probably blessed by the saint from a distance resulting in its pagan influence became inactive. Others explain that St Patrick appeared more interested in obtaining the cooperation of the powerful princely resident of Ros Airthir, brother of the High King of the time.

From the thirteenth century on, with the coming of the Anglo-Normans, this whole area of Oristown-Donaghpatrick become the preserve of the Knights Hospitallers of Kilmainham[102]. The fine modern church at Oristown, (R.C.) is today dedicated to Saint Catherine just as its forerunner in the nearby rath apparently also was. One may presume the new church replaces the ancient church or, more probably, several sequential ancient churches at Teltown since the early days of the Pale. The placing of an early church dedicated to Saint Catherine on the hill-top testifies to Anglo-Norman involvement (and just possibly to the canons of St Victor from Kells which see below) The residue (again, the 'blai an aonaigh') of paganism which the site

---

[101] See Prof. **Michael Herity** (Ed) *Ordnance Survey Letters -Meath* (Dublin 2001) Also importantly **Catherine Swift's** article *Oenach Tailten* in **Alfred P. Smith's** (Ed.) *Seanchas* (Dublin 2001) wherein she agrees with O'Donovan (p.11, ff.) as to the Ros Airthir site but also giving scholarly attention to the Telltown House site at pp114 and 116. See the Duchas Heritage Guide No.3 *Teltown* (Bray 1998)
[102] The Holy See confirmed *the Knights* Hospitallers of Kilrmainham <u>in</u> possession of the *lands of 'Douenachpatrick* and '*Kilteltan*' (evidently Teltown) by Decretal Letter dated 1212. (See **Maurice P. Sheehy's** *Pontificia Hibernica I p.149*)
[103] **Swift** (2000), already cited, points out that the Middle Irish *Senchas na Relec* identifies Teltown as an ancestral graveyard of the Ulaidh.

tended to retain (and which the clerics wished rid of), would have been the determining factor in the unusual location for a church. Its evident antiquity - the site of graves of the ancient heroes which it reputedly held – kept the people in thrall[103]. It also remains, however, equally needful to be considered how the central site for Aonach Tailtean as an alternative to that selected by **O'Donovan was discarded**. At least it must have been an important centre for fringe activities taking place after the preliminary ceremonies at Ros Airthir. The Teltown cemetery must have been for a long time an important pagan site holding as it did the bones of many well remembered from the mythological tales.

Saint Patrick (or whoever selected the Donaghpatrick site for an important church if not him.) did not evidently himself identify the hill-top site as the centre of the Teltown Assembly. Maire MacNeill appears not greatly surprised though she does not actually say so. Perhaps the hill-top was not a suitable site for a residence nor, having such a fearsome aura about it—until the hard–headed Anglo-Normans arrived— for a secondary church. Such matters are worthy of the attentions of archaeologistsand historians. It does not really concern this present 'exploration' except for it being necessary to examine whatever reasons there may be for the rather surprising Saint Catherine dedication.

The two possibilities then presenting themselves are (a) that it may have been Victorine canons from Kells who introduced the cult of the saint which they seem to have inherited from Bishop Thaddeus in the fifteenth century. This seems rather late and perhaps a somewhat esoteric solution which cannot however be ignored present itself. It will be returned to in detail in Chapter 17. (There, it will be argued that Saint Catherine may have been imaginatively used to substitute for a pagan entity—something not at all outside the capabilities of the Victorines though it may not have been of their ethos.)

INTERLUDE NO. 3

Hitherto matters, prior to 1500, have been given most attention, that is to say, following the introduction of the cult of Saint Catherine to Ireland in the thirteenth century, and its dissemination throughout the area where the English settled and become dominant. From the Lateran Council of 1215 the influence of the English ecclesiastics in all matters religious was felt especially strongly by the bishops supplied to Irish Dioceses and as prior abbots to Anglo-Norman priories /abbeys. The main purpose was the inculcating of the Irish the import of the Council Decrees. But, such intentions may have been resisted in practise, the Irish clerics often recognising them as of political intent rather than being genuinely religious.

Figure No. 16 The modern parish church of Saint Catherine of Alexandria
at Oristown, Co.Meath

For the great magnates, matters relating to conquest of the new lands and people certainly remained uppermost in their minds For the colonial ecclesiastics those Decrees were important which affected the native Irish Church (such as married clergy, erenaghts not in orders etc. Very many of the latter problems were actually being tackled in their own way by the Irish even before the Council condemned them). Ethnic differences within the dioceses and the monastic houses obtruded. The Irish quickly discerned when Anglicisation rather than religion was the real issue and soon such differences of attitude made themselves felt in the local churches. Then under the Reformation of Henry VIII and Elizabeth, some Decrees were countermanded while others were not, causing utter confusion amongst the native clergy.

Thereafter, while nowhere was Saint Catherine's cult specifically outlawed, her images and offerings at her shrines were discouraged, as being 'profane'[104] The old enthusiasm for the cults waned. Some earlier dedications of churches, however were kept along with the buildings which survived. New churches on old sites often preserved the old dedications. But, for those clerics who continued in allegiance to the old church, they and their congregations went to open-air masses at rocky altars and Holy Wells. The non Irish saints also perhaps tended to be forgotten. The penitential sites became popular again and some almost forgotten Irish saints' pilgrimages were resurrected.

A further prolongation of cults into the post -medieval period took place largely through the efforts of the canons regular and the mendicant friars from their dispersed convents. Such places as Croagh Patrick, Saint Patrick's Purgatory (Lough Derg), Ventry, and Saint Catherine's Well, Killybegs, played their part in supplying ancient rituals in competition with what the Reformers offered against Rome. Saint Catherine's cult thrived at only a few. In Dublin city St. Thomas's Court was secularised by the Puritans and went into decline. There and in other cities and the bigger towns the Neo-Romans turned to undistinguished dwelling houses for the saying of masses and even for hiding order priests' dwellings and convents. Not many late Roman Catholic dedications to Saint Catherine were made. Only those preserved at Meath Street or Ochterlin for example, may be noted. Saint Catherine's name may have been substituted at Holy Wells. One suspects that the granting of the site for the R.C. Church in Meath Street by the Earl of Meath contained a stipulation that it should be dedicated to the same saint whose ancient church once existed in nearby Hanbury Lane. (See Map No. 2 above) No doubt its building was intended for Roman Catholics who were being 'persecuted' by the 'Liberty Boys' The church on Thomas Street for the episcopalians was built ("begun") in 1765 to replace a former unsuitable 'St.Catherine's' from pre Reformation times.

---

[104] See **Dudley Edward's** *Church and State in Tudor Ireland* (Dublin 1935) pp.22,23,148.

CHAPTER NO 13

The cult of Saint Catherine in the dioceses of Raphoe and Clogher

There are four medieval sites in th herein mentioned dioceses dedicated to Saint Catherine, three whose origin may be reasonably well inferred and a third comprising the Holy Well and a ruined and partly reused church site at Killybegs for which detailed discussion will be required. There is some difficulty with this last in tracking it either directly or indirectly, back to the Anglo-Normans for the Anglo-Normans as such did not enter successfully into Tir Conaill. (County Donegal) Their successors, the English, however, finally did so in the fifteenth century when they initially penetrated the area about Sligo and Ballyshannon to the south. Inishowen and the north eastern parts, had been largely abandoned by the Anglo-Norman Lords of Ulster in the fourteenth century, leaving just a few small settlements in Lough Foyle and the castle of Neuburg / Greencastle. (to-day a hardly imposing ruin.) The Raphoe diocese even into late medieval times may be considered to have been free from outside civil authority.

A reference in the Annals to a matter not appearing at first sight to be of any great moment or historical importance, occurs for the year 1513. It refers to a raid by pirates on the town of Killybegs, which mentions Saint Catherine as providing protection for the town against such perpetrators—since, according to **O'Donovan**,the editor of one of the Annals, she had this duty as the towns patron. In what follows an attempt will be made to show that this was not quite correct for the time when the raid occurred. The implications this literary judgement has on the history of the cult at Killybegs are considerable but need not lead to any diminution in the sites attractiveness for Roman Catholics and other devotees. The saint certainly became patron of the town and parish later than the aforementioned date but the saint only came under particular notice in or about the time ca 1600 when the Annals for the period were being compiled and brought up to date.

The pirate raid was considered worthy of mention in each of the four important Annals by the Four Masters[105], of Ulster[106], of Connacht.[107] and of Lough Key,[108] but only in AFM and AU is mention made of the intervention of Saint Catherine in the event. **O'Donovan** in the annotation of his Annals declares her to have been Patron of the town at the time. **Hennessy** editor of simply refers to Saint Catherine as having appeared in **Gorman's** *Calendar.*

In this present writing it is posited that the raid on Killybegs took place on the 25th November, the Feast Day of Saint Catherine of Alexandria in 1513. The omission of this salient fact caused **O'Donovan** to ascribe Patronage of the saint of Killybegs, somewhat too early. It was only when Toirdealbhach, her son, founded the Third Order Franciscan Friary that people sat up and took notice according her the honour she was due. By recognising this a number of anomalies arising in the narrations disappear. A little further information on the life of Máire may assist the reader in these issues and will now be provided.

---

[105] **John O' Donovan** *(Ed)* 7 Vols Second Edition, (Dublin 1856) Henceforth 'AFM'

[106] **W.M.Hennessy and B. McCarthy** (Eds.) (Dublin 1887 - 1901) Henceforth AU

[107] **A. Martin Freeman** (Ed) (Dublin 1944) says two ships taken) Henceforth ACon..

[108] **W. M. Hennessy**(Ed) 2Vols, (Dublin 1871 Reprint 2000) Henceforth ALCé.

[109] In an O.S. Letter (1835) par 230 Donegal Letters, **O'Donovan** suggested Catherine was a corruption of Carthach the patron saint of Kilcar. If he had said Ciarán of Saidhir, Carthach's bishop, the comparison of sounds would have been closer. Two miles from Killybegs is Ciaran's Holy well. (at Bavin - See *Lockard and O'Callaghan 2001 p.76*) The present write, believes it probable the Saint Catherines Well's name as substituted for St Ciarán only becoming "Saint Catherine's" Well after the issue of the Irish Life of Saint Catherine

Figure No 17 Ruins of 'Saint Catherine's Third Order Franciscan Friary' at Killybegs. (Much altered and added to by the Plantation Settlers in the seventeenth Century.)

It has been identified as the remains of a Friary (by **Lacy et al** who describe it as "of fifteenth century". This is disputed herein for historical reasons.

Máire Ní Mháille, wife of Ruidhrí Mac Suibhne Chief of Fanad

It is worthwhile recounting a contemporary statement referring to this lady. It appears in an document composed shortly after her death, *'An Craobhscaoileadh Chlainne Suibhne,'* in which Maire is styled "the most generous and the best mother and the woman of most fame in regard to faith. and piety of all who lived in her time."[110] She was a fervent devotee of Saint Catherine of Alexandria and caused a Latin Life of the saint to be translated into Irish.[111] This manuscript Life (part of the aforementioned *Craobhscaoileadh*), is held by the Royal Irish Academy, Dublin and is referred to in Rev. **Paul Walsh's** *'Book of the MacSweeneys'*. It dates from early 1500s probably immediately after the aforementioned raid. It provides authentic information (in large part, much earlier than AFM) of Maire's origin and career. The large endowments that Maire made to Rathmullan Friary were in memory of her son Ruidhrí who is buried there. The nearby present-day chapel - of - ease at Ochterlin, in the parish of Rathmullan, was dedicated to Saint Catherine of Alexandria in 1792, a circumstance which has given rise to some puzzlement.[112]

---

[110] The following is excerpted from *Craobhscaoileadh* (P.Walsh's translation from *The Book of the MacSweeneys* p 67) in further relation to Máire and her husband, Chief Ruidhrí.

This is the manner in which she passed her days. She used to hear Mass once a day and sometimes more than once; and three days of each week she used to spend on bread and water fare, with Lenten Fast and winter fast and the Golden Fridays. She also caused to be erected a Great Hall for the Friar's Minor in Dun na nGall. Not only that but many other churches we shall not here enumerate that woman caused to be built in The Provinces of Ulster and Connacht.

The following were the children of that couple...Ruidhrí Óg..he was the elder son... he died [in 1508]... and was buried in the church of Rath Maoilain... it was mainly on account of that the monastery was erected... Ruidhrí[0g] left no descendants...Toirdealbhach was the second son.. and was Mac Suibhne Chief of Fanad. {There is knowledge from tradition of an elder son, Conor, who resigned the Chieftainship and entered the Carmalites.}

[111] It is to be found in R.I.A. Ms 24 P 25. **Gearoid Mac Niocaill** has deciphered the difficult writing (See APPENDIX 4, a digitised facsimile reproduction of one page) He has edited the text, supplying it in contemporary Irish in *Eigse* 8 (1956-57) p. 232-35 In an introduction he gives the date of the manuscript as 1513-4, describing it as a translation from an unidentified Latin source —: *Beatha agus Bas Chaithreach Fina* by **Ciothruadh Magh Fhionnghaill** from Tory Island. As an addition to the usual legend it has the author suggesting that Catherine was a child of the Emperor's harem and was attracted by her youthful beauty. This seems to add a degree of verisimilitude to the standard version.

Another Irish language *Life* is to be found in the British Library. Listed by **Robin Flower** in his *Catalogue of Irish Manuscripts (1926). it is f*rom Galway; dated 1726. Known as Egerton Gaelic 184, it may be seen on microfilm at NLI. T.C.D also has an early Life in Irish numbered H.2.17,p.29 dated 1484 which may be from the Latin'Vulgate ' version. It is suggested by Flower to be the origin for RIA Ms 24 P 25 A poem extracted (?) from the latter occurs in the *Book of the Dean of Lismore*, Scotland, written in about 1512-1529 according to **Flower**. (**Katherine Lewis** (2000) gives an account of the eleventh century Latin 'Vulgate ' version at p.9)

[112] **Rev. John J. Silke's** *The Diocese of Raphoe* (2000) has a photograph. Maire Ni Mhaille wife of the Chief of Fanad whose residence was nearby, introduced devotion to Saint Catherine from Mayo in early sixteenth century. The priest who named this church **Rev. McElwee** must have had some knowledge of this from tradition. Maire is interred bside Ruidhrí her son at Rathmullan Priory. There are few remnants of this site remaining.

The Mac Sweeney Clan - Gallowglass Mercenaries of the Irish Chieftains

Clann Suibhne were widely distributed in Ireland and provided military service for a wide range of Lordships some of whom may be opposed one against the other. At the beginning of the 16th century it is unlikely that the three groups in Tir Conaill, Mac Suibhne (of Fanad') and Mac Suibhne ('of Banagh') were at one on local matters or even on friendly terms. (Their loyalty to O Domhnaill was, of course, undeniable.)

The Mac Suibhne Clan derived their ancestry from different Scottish origins, the Banagh branch coming to Tír Conaill from Connacht only since mid-fourteenth century. Mac Suibhne Connachtach, their close relatives, were serving, at the beginning of the sixteenth century, as gallowglass mercenaries to the Clanriocaird/MacWilliam Burkes in Galway, Mayo and most of Sligo, at least up to ca.1515, Clannriocaird had been sharing the wealth of the town of Sligo with O Domhnaill, an arrangement not at all to the latter's liking. In 1461 O Domhnaill had settled an accord with the three Tír Conaill Mac Suibhne gallowglass families , securing their joint loyalty to him. Whether friendship existed across Donegal Bay between these Tír Conaill families and those of Connacht (that is to say including MacSuibhne Connachtach and the O'Malleys of County Mayo, another mercenary family) one may not be certain. Marriage settlements between the O'Malleys and Mac Suibhne (Fanad) are noted in '*Craobhscaoileadh*' and were calculated to copperfasten a sort of friendship between them. Two marriages on record between the families of special interest, were firstly Onóra Ní Mháille's who married Ruidhrí Mac Suibhne (the eldest son of Chief Toirdealbhach of Fanad, then tánaiste), while Máire Ní Mháille married another Ruidhrí, son of Maolmhuire Mac Suibhne. (This Ruidhri became Chief ahead of his normal successor, his cousin the tánaiste, when the old Toirdealbhach died.)[113]

---

[113] See *Craobhscaoileadh* pars 41, 4, 49. This Toirdealbhach, son of Ruidhrí and Maire, became Chief of Fanad in 1528. He died in 1544 or -45,- (See **J.F. Quinn's** *History of Mayo* 11 p. 113 (reprint Ballina 1993) **Quinn** says he died in Bunishoole, his mother's home Clearly the loss of the chieftainship to Ruidhri by Onora's husband still rankled and resulted in kin -slaying, the curse of the system. (To her sons it had been a bitter blow and had the (later) consequence of Toirdealbhach being driven out while severely wounded by them following personal combat. The founder of Killybegs Friary died of his wounds shortly afterwards, having been brought to his mother's people in Mayo to die).

Nothing is known of arrangements of the same type between the Tír Conaill MacSuibhne families, Fanad and Banagh, or MacSuibhne Connachtach; Presumably these were not entered into, on the assumption that filial ties should be sufficient. The O'Malleys (Irish form "Ó Máille") were, however, under obligation to the MacWilliam Burkes Íochtarach, and could well be required to render service to the related Clanriocaird branch of that clan. Indeed the occasion of the aforementioned marriages was probably expected to deter them from such, as Ó Domhnaill was contemplating proceeding against the Clanriocairds in Sligo. He more than likely had such plans in mind without notifying the families thus joined with his blessing. (Hugh Ruadh Ó Domhnaill's - reputation is not very good in such matters).

Any suggestion of playing false would be badly received in Fanad, conflicting as it would be with the spirit of the marriages. How badly it would be taken by the other members of the clan one cannot be sure as they were not a very cohesive group. When it did happen, however, and O'Malley went with Clanriocard in ca.1512, there must have been consternation amongst the Mac Suibhne Chief's family in Fanad who would have known of Ó Domhnaill's plans. Ó Domhnaill began the seige of Sligo in March 1513 (when one of the kin of the Fanad gallowglass clan was killed) No doubt Chief Ruidhri was present during this action also. Máire's worries then were about her husband and her relatives in combat on both sides She had already lost her first born, also a Ruidhrí, five years before. (The siege went on desultorily until 1516.) Because of business elsewhere (See AFM for 1513 to 1518) Ó Domhnaill withdrew temporarily from Sligo. Clanriocaird then, taking the opportunity to strengthen his forces, called upon Owen O' Malley, who had many sea going galleys at his disposal, for assistance. Daringly, Owen decided to make a raid on Killybegs while Niall Mór Mac Suibhne Chief of Banagh was engaged on the Ó Domhnaill activities elsewhere. He succeeded in pressing many recruits for Clanriocaird at Killybegs but a storm drove the ships back on shore as they were leaving Before they could get away again, a nephew of Niall Mor was able to gather some young non-combatants together and by causing a fire and helped by the high wind they succeeded in diverting the attention of Owen and his men who were come on land. By this stratagem the prisoners were freed and two of the galleys sunk, only one getting away according to one report. The leader of the foray, Owen O' Malley lost his life, that is, the captain of the galleys who was brother of Máire.

Máire, besides grieving over the death of her brother also suffered the indignity of familial connection with the Killybegs raider. This impacted on herself since her loyalty to her Mac Suibhne family was thereby impugned. It was brought home even more upon her head when Niall Mór MacSuibhne, Chief of Banagh, on his returning from the wars heard the reason for the galleys being in Killybegs was for the purpose of taking on board recruits for Clanriocaird. He made no end of a fuss possibly to broadcast his delight with his young nephew's success. But Máire at hearing of her brother Owen's death felt his offence against her extended family most keenly. In her view it would require the help of one of the great saints in heaven to save his soul, together with the prayers of many friars. Later, understanding that his oath to his overlord made it imperative to act as he did, she perhaps forgave him his personal hurt to her.

The account given above is an elaboration of that provided by AFM. We now come to a coincidence which may however be explained (if explanation be needed) for some confusion of entries during its compilation. The Annals of the Four Masters, especially in regard to their pre 1000 entries, were prone to duplications and probably were here also. An entry for the kin-slaying of Ó Domhnaill's son and heir at "Tuath-bhleadhach," (an important occurrence which took place probably in one of the Three Tuaths) is entered for 1515, (two years after the Killybegs event). Interestingly, it is mentioned as having taken place on 25th of November without, however, stating that this was the feast of Saint Catherine Such accurate dating was not common in the Annals except for especially important events. The scribe may have cast about for a date for this one. Finding one two years before which seemed surplus to requirements, he seems to have abstractedly adapted it for his purpose without making the necessary retrospective changes to the text.

By providing this explanation two difficulties are removed, firstly disposing of the coincidence and secondly the rather easy **O'Donovan's** crediting Saint Catherine with the patronage of Killybegs earlier than deserved. It besides fits better with the falling out of events succeeding the death of Maire. The saint was really deemed deserving of the honour of patronage of the town only when Máire drew attention to her powerful efficacy in general by issuing her Irish *Life of Saint Catherine*. By using it so soon after the raid on Killybegs only presented an anomalous fact for the Annals' scribe to endeavour to fit (which he did but with an inevitable contradiction). He reacted by omitting any reference to the Irish life of Saint Catherine, a matter which cried out for mention.)

The evidence thus adduced is consistent with the timing proposed below for the founding of the Franciscan Third Order Friary in Killybegs by Maire's son, Chief Toirdealbhach, that is in about 1535-40. There is little doubt that it was done in her name and this writer has no hesitation in proposing it while considering the facts implied by the above.

It is not intended to suggest that there was no knowledge of Saint Catherine in the Killybegs area before the early sixteenth century. There is ample evidence that indeed there was. A penitential bed in her name existed at Lough Derg by 1480 at latest. One Caitlín (Catherine), daughter of Mac Suibhne (Chief of Fanad) is recorded in AFM as having died in 1530. She was wife of O'Doherty, presumably Chief of an Inishowen Tuath. She must have been born towards the end of the fifteenth century. It is not impossible she was a daughter of Máire herself but perhaps more likely was given the name at baptism by her as Chief's wife. At any rate it may be taken that the saint was quite popular throughout Tír Conaill at the time. Yet she did not deserve the title of "Patron" until the *Life* in the vernacular appeared.

How Máire Ní Mháille may have become imbued of the Catherine Cult

The Victorine Canons Regular ceased to have reason to continue in existence in their original form from about 1450. Even the larger abbeys for Augustinian canons were already in decline by that time. Many canons had already left the smaller houses to join the mendicant friars or the Cistercians, abandoning the Augustinian Rule as outdated. The new Order of Augustinian Hermits became Friars in the fifteenth century and provided an outlet for many retiring canons.

In exploring how Máire developed her attachment to Saint Catherine it is necessary to look at her home district on the shores of Clew Bay in Mayo, where, shortly before she was born, a new foundation for Augustinian Friars was begun at Murrisk. (For a long time it was the official site for beginning the Pilgrimage to Croagh Patrick). The land for building this Friary was granted by Tadhg O'Malley, chief of his sept. Tadhg was father of Diarmaid Bacach O'Malley, the father of Máire. Clearly there was a strong religious tradition in that family. According to **Gwynn and Hadcock-,** the actual foundation of Murrisk was instigated by "Lady" Maeve O'Connor, wife of Diarmaid Bacach.

Bearing such an appellation, Lady Maeve was probably one of those O'Connors who claimed descent from the royal line of the kings of Connacht, beginning with Cathal Crobhderg O'Connor in the thirteenth century. Females of this line were famously pious. Many of them ended their lives in the great convent of Kilcreevanty near Tuam, several of them becoming abbesses there. It may be concluded that through her mother Maeve, that Maire received her devotion to Saint Catherine and perhaps was bequeathed that valuable Latin manuscript *Life of Saint Catherine,* mentioned above. It would have come down in a similar manner of decent to lady Maeve via several antecedent sisters in religion under the auspices of Kilcreevanty. Maire, as we know, had it translated from the Latin at Rathmullen by a monk / scribe from Tory Island [114]

Figure No 18 Bridgetown Priory, Co. Cork

---

[114] (a)It is noteworthy that the commission to undertake the translation was given to the scribe **Mac Fhionnghaill** in 1513 to be completed within a year. Maire clearly planned straight away after the death of Owen to promote devotion to Saint Catherine of Alexandria through he Irish Life and its circulation.

(b) By the time that AFM was complied in the early seventeenth century, the cult of Saint Catherine was at full strength at her Holy Well at Killybegs, Even the incoming Plantation settlers had not rejected her. They set up their Reformed religion, and built their church under the name of Saint Catherine. The Holy Well had been recently consecrated by a foreign bishop (see Chapter 17 below) and pilgrima were coming in numbers. How was it that AFM failed to mention Máire Ni Mháille, wife of Ruidhri Mac Suibhne, Chief of Fanad and the part she played in the whole affair? Had her memory become lost and the puerile account of 1513 been forced upon the annalists because of the evident popularity of the traditional rites being performed by the pilgrims at the well following on an evident tradition requiring a very ready explanation?

CHAPTER 14

The cult of Saint Catherine in the archdiocese of Tuam and the diocese of Clonfert

It is not possible to say if Victorine canons ever crossed the river Shannon into Connacht, but it is very probable that clerics influenced by them and bringing the devotion of Saint Catherine with them did so. There is evidence for it. There were Aroassian canons from about 1150 in the province- Some of them continued to occupy various priories and houses right up to the 'Henrician' Dissolution (which came there rather late, It was mostly Elizabethan in Connacht) Right up to the seventeenth century canons were being presented to neighbouring nunneries for the saying of mass. Aroassian / Benedictine canonesses took to the cult easily. The large convent of Kilcreevanty which was near the seat of the primatial see of Tuam had already achieved a degree of provincial status when adopted by Pope Honorius III in 1223.[115] His indult lists sixty convents in charge of the Abbess of Kilcreevanty throughout Connacht.

Rev. **Patrick Egan**, in his *History of the Parish of Ballinasloe,* states there were three convents of canonesses in the diocese of Clonfert, one of which, at Aughrim was dedicated to Saint Catherine. (The Calendar of Papal Letters for '1509 has reference to an "O.S.A Priory of Aughrim dedicated to Saint Catherine") As Saint Catherine sometimes displaced the Blessed Virgin Mary (or 'Saint Mary') in dedications one need not suppose that her names absence from the few surviving documents proves a lack of popularity of Saint Catherine's cult within the walls of the convents or especially in the Kilcreevanty province.[116] The unlikely finding of an effigy of the saint in fragile wood from Kilcorban, ("The Tynagh Saint Catherine") testifies to this.[117] Egan notes that Clontuskert Priory had six parishes, including Aughrim, to which it supplied canons.[118] The high regard with which Saint Catherine was held at Clontuskert is displayed by the sculptured effigy of the saint along with Saints Michael and John the Baptist which remain today above the arched doorway of the ruined church there. (For an Illustration see Leask(1960) plateX)[119]

[115] *Pontificia Hibernicia* Vol I p.239

[116] The ruined Clontuskert friary as seen today, is fully described: by **Leask** in his *Irish Churches and Monastic Buildings* (Dundalk 1960) Part III p 75 **Peter Harrison** has a fine photograph in his *Church Heritage in East Galway* p.48

[117] It is preserved in the diocesan museum at Loughrea and is illustrated in **Rev. Egan's** *Clonfert Museum and its Collections* in *Galway Archaeological and Historical Society's Journal* (1947 – 1948)

[118] (Already cited) at p 29 and 30

[119] See **Leask**, already cited, Vol. III p 74.. The Church of Ireland parish church of Aghascragh, not far from Aughrim is dedicated to Saint Catherine.

Finally, to confirm her antecedent patronage still further; in Máire Ni Mháille's own county attention is drawn to what remains of the Dominican abbey of Burrishoole. Nearby used to be a nunnery of Tertiaries, (of an unknown Order,} of which Sister Honora Burke was a young member. Before the end of the sixteenth century, suppression had been ordered. by the Elizabethan Commission. But this nunnery was still active as the Queen Elizabeth's Commissioners could not come in. However, Sir Richard Maltby, the Commissioner for Connacht, made his way into the locality in 1580 under strict orders of leniency. As the Commissioner and his soldiers made their way to the area, the nuns ran off, only Honora Burke, remaining. She escaped by hiding in the Parish Church nearby (The old church was replaced by the Newport C.O.I. church but this has since been rebuilt elsewhere. All of these churches and sites are and are dedicated to Saint Catherine of Alexandria). The old site was taken over at the Reformation and there seems no doubt it originated from the time of Máire Ní Mháille's parents.[120]

---

[120] Information gleaned from **Gwynn and Hadcock** p.222 also from **E.A-Brandon's** *To Whom we Dedicated* (Dublin 1971). Honora is remembered for having been murdered much later by Cromwellian soldiery (in 1653). See **Eamonn Burke's** *Burke People and Places* 4th Edition (Dublin 2001) pp32, 33.

CHAPTER 15

The cult of Saint Catherine in the Dioceses of Ferns and Ossory

The ruined Church of Nook

The principal site in the Diocese of Ferns devoted to Saint Catherine is at Nook near Duncannon. It is located on the shores of Waterford Harbour but well inside its mouth. The connection with this unlikely saint is presumed to have arisen from its having been a Grange of Saint Catherine's Abbey, Waterford. The abbey's estates in the diocese of Waterford occupied a large part of the ancient parish of Saint Catherine (otherwise Grange Upper, now Killea) This lay across the harbour in County Waterford from Nook. The extent of this medieval parish is mentioned and mapped by **Canon Power** in his *Placenames of the Decies* (2nd Ed.Cork 1952).[121] The map shows the Parish extending down to the shore at Passage East on the County Waterford side of the Harbour just opposite Nook on the County Wexford side.

The site of the ruins of this Saint Catherine's Chapel is located on the banks of that part of the estuary known as 'Saint Catherine's Bay'. This is at the confluence of the three rivers, the Suir, the Nore and the Barrow. In pagan times such places were deemed of great sanctity. Somewhere about the place of joining several tributaries confluence, a 'nematon' or place of prayer to the gods, was commonly located.[122] If this was such a site, as is not at all improbable, a re-sanctification of Nook would have taken place upon the arrival of Christianity. Inevitably upon the arrival of the Anglo-Normans the native saint (perhaps the great local Ruadhan) had, as usual, to give way to one favoured by the settlers. According to **O'Donovan**, it was called "Buttermilk Castle" (Caislean na Blathaighe) but it does not appear as such in the Ordnance Survey Maps.

---

[121] **Canon Power's** map (page 224) is adapted from the Down Survey
[122] A junction of two great rivers would have impressed prehistoric invaders. This junction was later called 'Cumar na dTri nUisge' and later still 'Saint Catherine's Bay' (See **O'Donovan** Wexford Letters)

When du Noyer, the noted antiquarian artist, visited the site in the 1860 he prepared excellent drawings of what he saw. Some of these ruins, though further decayed, remain standing today.[123] Du Noyer noted a niche in the wall nearest the river bank of the ruined church, which he interpreted as a lamp - stand for a torch to aid boats coming in at dusk after leaving a landing place (perhaps that near Cheekpoint on the other side in County Waterford.)

A contributor to JRSAI described the ruins in 1912 when preparing for a visit of the Society to Waterford. He mentions a Saint Catherine's Holy Well near the site. This is now sadly neglected, but could perhaps be recovered with the help of the local landowner At the Henrician Dissolution, the site at Nook ('Nowegg"), then known as 'Saint Catherine's church', was appropriate to Dunbrody Abbey, three miles away.[124] A mound, or, in the word of the historian **Hore,** 'a prominence', would have been presumed by an early missioner to require Christianisation and "occupation of the site by a primitive cell". **Hore** in his History gives a good account of Nook,and its foundation. It is illustrated by a fine Du Noyer drawing which shows some slight differences from today. (See Figure 19 below).[125] Of probably fourteenth century origin, all commentators view it as having been a fortified house of religion. but "They, agree about its having a secondary function as a lookout base over an important waterway"

---

[123] JRSAI \ JKSEIAS 1864

[124] Cistercian, See JRSAI 1912 p.268

[125] **P.Hore's** *History of the Town and County of Wexford Vol.III pp.250-6*. Simon W. Kennedy, New Ross, has kindly drawn attention to this site and provided other information and photographs of the Parish of Ramsgrange

---

Figure No 19 A view (1871) of the ruined Church of Nook at Saint Catherine's Bay, Wexford. (from **Hore's** *History of Wexford* using Du Noyer's Sketch)

The ruined Nook church is in the Roman Catholic parish of Saint James and Saint Catherine. The parish church is in the village of Ramsgrange, County Wexford and diocese of Ferns it has a small stained glass windows showing both saints. The church at Duncannon, in the same parish, also has representations of Saints Catherine and James but somewhat larger. (See Figure 21a. at p.115)

There is another curious Desmond connection by Inquisition 1578, Maurice Fitzgerald, Lord Decies (d. 1572) was found in occupation of lands of Dunbrody Abbey including Nook, Dungarvan and Ring (ogonaigh) and after his death by his brother James (d. 1581). It Seems Saint Catherine was associated with them somehow (see footnote 82).

Parts of County Wexford were intensely settled by the Anglo-Normans. An effort seems to have been made to eradicate the old Irish saints attached to church sites and to replace them with their own. The bishops of Ferns (who had not been consecrated in Canterbury!) about the turn of the century -1200- were reluctant to give way in the matter. We have an account of a bishop excommunicating Lord Marshal (who had married Strongbow's daughter Isabella) and refusing to withdraw his ruling even after Marshal's death.

At Tacumshin Bay the rites accorded to Saint Munnu Fintan were found difficult to put an end to even by the Anglo- Normans. Having extended the church, formerly dedicated to the Irish saint, they wished to re-dedicate it to Saint Catherine. The new dedication however proved only partially successful as the Pattern transferred to the adjoining Holy Well, continuing on 21st October, the feast day of Saint Munnu.[126]

---

[126] The editors of *The Archaeological Inventory of County Wexford* (Dublin 1999) describe the church site as "Saint Catherine's Abbey, Tacumshin" but did not mention the Holy Well. For this reference must be made to **Edward Culleton's** *Celtic and Early Christian Wexford* p. 39 (map and p. 214). **O'Donovan** mentions a well dedicated to St Ivor at Buttlerstown known to have been re-dedicated to St. Catherine

The Church of Ireland church at Toome near Camolin, was also dedicated to Saint Catherine. **O'Donovan** has a sketch of the remains of the Church 1848 in his *Wexford Letters* 1par.24

A Calendar case at Rathbeagh Parish, Co. Kilkenny. (Diocese of Ossory)

In 1582 Pope Gregory XIII took the initiative in rectifying an imbalance which had taken place between the Calendar and the seasons since Julius Caesar had fixed it.[127] The Pope directed that ten days be added but this did not come into force in the Protestant countries until 1752 when it was necessary to add extra days, thus September 2nd 1652 was called "September 13th". Christmastime was found difficult to surrender and thus the new 4th January (principally in Irish-speaking districts) becoming 'Nollaig na mBan' or 'Little Christmas', later the people combined the old season with The Epiphany in a combination holiday. (The Epiphary was an ancient feast day also called Twelfth Night - almost coincidental)

In the Gaeltacht also, some other festivals continued to be celebrated with ancient rituals on the New calendar date but ten days later "Until recently. St Bridget's day (Imbolc) on the 11th February (on St. Gobnat's Day) and All Saints' day (Samhain) on 11th November (on St. Martin's Day) were carefully remembered in Irish-speaking areas of Munster on the new dates until recently. Moreover, the battle of the Boyne (1st July) was accepted by Protestants as the '12th July' but the old date still remains in the ancestral memory

At 'Rathbeagh,' parish, Co. Kilkenny, **John O'Donovan** in his *Ordnance Survey Letters*,[128] noted (1835) a church ruin and Holy Well dedicated to Saint Catherine. Her feast day being celebrated as a 'day of obligation through 'obligatory practises for Saint Catherine's Feast had ceased long before, nearly to his surprise, the feast day was being held on sixth of January — eleven days after 25th November. (The year 1600 was not a year requiring an extra day to be added but 1700 and 1800 were) Evidently the revised sixteenth century calendar date of pope Gregory XIII had not been adopted at Rathbeagh. The obligatory duties for a Holy Day, considered every where else to have been waived by Papal Decree, at Rathbeagh parish continued to be observed. Perhaps the information had not penetrated to the area or it was deliberately ignored, but the old obligations were religiously observed when **O'Donovan** visited there.

---

[127] See Note on Dating p.(xv) in **Moody, Martin and O'Byrne's** *New History of Ireland* Vol IX

[128] See **Michael Herity(Ed.)** *Ordnance Survey Letters Kilkenny* (Dublin 2003) par. 88 See also **Seamus O Cathain** 's *The Festival of Brigit* (Blackrock 1995)

Callan., Co Kilkenny. (Diocese of Ossory)

In the town of Callan,Co Kilkenny the C.O.I. church in Main Street comprises buildings old and new The oldest part at the rear (called by **Samuel Lewis** in his **Dictionary** 'the ante- chapel') was in ruins in Lewis time but it probably represented part of a thirteenth century church of the canons regular of St. Augustine of the community of St. Victor. There are two artefacts dedicated to Saint Catherine which supply evidence for this statement. One is the sculpture (depicting the saint with her wheel - see figure on page 81- in the cemetary. Another as stated by **O' Donovan** was a chantry altar in the chapel dedicated to The Holy Trinity and Saint Catherine (There may have been two) "for the purpose of saying mass for the repose of the souls of the noble family of Desart" There is also in the town a ruined Friary of the Augustinian Order, not to be confused with the earlier canons chapel now part of the C.O.I Church. (The present writer was unable to obtain entry to this church when visiting the area).

CHAPTER 16

**Miscellaneous other sites:- Holy Wells, etc., associated
with Saint Catherine and some not dedicated in her name.**

Saint Mary's (Bridgetown) Priory, Castletownroche, County Cork

Located at an apparently early bridge over the river Black-water, near
Castletownroche,this site is noted here even though (while being Victorine) it is not
dedicated to Saint Catherine.[129] It is one of the few ruined Augustinian priories which
can be contemplated in the whole, Its site is quite large, the lack of roofing over the
various elements being its major defect. Being in this condition for over four
hundred years has been disastrous for the fabric. It was a foundation originally supplied
with canons from distant Newtown –Trim, County Meath [130] also called Saint Mary's.

Bridgetown Abbey was founded, ca. 1207 (doubtless being supplied with canons
provided from Waterford Abbey as well as Newtown-Trim. It seems coincidental
that it was about this year also that the headship of the see of Meath transferred to
Newtown/Trim. One suspects that with the completion of the Cathedral the canons
were no longer needed there and an opportunity was seized for their building skills
to be utilised elsewhere.

A possible explanation for Saint Catherine's name not being associated with either
of these two Victorine priories, Newtown Trim and Bridgetown, may be that they
were not located in Hiberno-Norse districts. These Norman canons probably felt
somewhat alien amongst the Irish population. The Priory was again empty almost
for a century, seemingly after a plague. When repopulated in the fifteenth century it
was at a time when only non-Irish canons were permitted. Furthermore, a native
Irish saint was popular amongst the people of the area - Saint Findchua of Brigowen,
near Mitchelstown, less than twenty miles away. He had his Feast-day also on 25th
November - the same as Saint Catherine.

---

[129] See **T.O'Keeffe's**. *Bridgetown Priory An Anglo-Norman Monastery:* (Kinsale *1999)* This present writer cannot
resist speculating that the skilled canons from Newtown Trim were brought there because of their skill at bridge
–building. A bridge at Bridgetown was urgently needed at the time to get from Dublin and Limerick to Cork.
See **A.M.McCormack's** *The Eerldom of Desmond* (Dublin 2005) p.36. It was never built.

[130] See **Gwynn and Hadcock**.p.161-2

Paradoxically there is no masonry bridge at Bridgetown of the same age. One is tempted to surmise an early translation of canons from Newtown - Trim to Bridgetown anticipating the final decision of the Dublin governors in the matter of the best route to Cork, The final one taken was that the route over the Nangle Hills by Bridgetown should be abandoned. The loss of tolls would have been serious for the Priory and effected it later.

Tadhg O'Keefe in his book (Kinsale 1990) shows how he investigated the adjacent lands from the Air for hidden structures but without success. Neither did any abandoned approach - roads towards a prospective bridge site appear. **O'Keefe** reference to the granting of toll rights to the Priory seems to have been also anticipatory. (p.36) The early medieval (thirteenth century) bridge over the Awbeg at Buttevant may have replaced it. (The kind suggestion of a knowledgeable informant, Mr Christy Roche of Fermoy)

Saint Catherine's Bed at Lough Derg, (that is at St Patrick's penitential Purgatory, County Donegal, in the diocese of Clogher)

It has often been wondered by those who attend this pilgrimage (for it is still popular) how one of the stations there came by its name — 'Saint Catherine's Bed', called after a non-Irish saint. Some suppose it to be dedicated to Saint Catherine of Siena, which however is not correct. The history of this extraordinary and long-lived penitential station has recently been examined by **Michael Haren**, and **Yoldand de Pontfarcy with others**.[131]

There was no mention of Saint Catherine's Bed in the many accounts of the Purgatory recorded prior to 1497, at which time the site was demolished on the instructions of Pope Innocent VIII. (The Bull was issued by Pope Alexander VI) The former observances were shortly afterwards transferred by the Augustinian (Aroassian) canons in charge of the Purgatory, from Saint Dabheoc's (or 'Saints') Island to Station Island where it is to-day. (Saints' Island having become tainted with the sin of simony by Pope Alexander's Bull. The banning of the entire pilgrimage followed a complaint by a canon from Eymstadt who was disappointed after undertaking the long and difficult journey to it at not experiencing the demons promised). Station Island was soon afterwards formally absolved.[132]

Early clochan cells which survived on Station Island but were collapsed were used as new 'stations" or 'beds' and bore similar attributions as the former beds of Saints' Island. Saint Catherine's name, though not yet established as patron at nearby Killybegs,(see page 88 herein) was certainly known on Saints' Island for a a penitential station, and was continued as such on Station Island.[133] Though nothing is heard of it before its appearance on **Thomas Carve's** Map of 1666, in her book **de Pontfarcy** (at page 80) quotes **William Caxton** telling how he met a canon from Waterford in 1480— no doubt from the Victorine congregation there- who had attended the Pilgrimage six times. The frequency of his patronage was astonishing for a time when travel was so perilous. (Two or more normally travelled together.) The considerable number of visits undertaken by this canon connotes some proprietary interest by Waterford Abbey - perhaps in the installation or preservation of Saint Catherine's name at the Pilgrimage site.

---

[131] *The Medieval Pilgrimage to Saint Patrick's Purgatory* (Enniskillen 1988) See also *Ulster Local Studies* (Belfast Winter 1993) *Pre Reformation Pilgrimages to St.Patrick's Purgatory* by **Yolande de Pontfarcy (1985)**

[132] The suppression of the Purgatory occurred in 1497, (The transfer of activities to the *new* site occurred after the condemnation was revoked by Rome in 1522.)

[133] The printer William Caxton writing about that time i.e. 1480, in his *Mirror of the World* had met the canon from Waterford prior to that date.

Arguments which might be in favour of presented for the presence in the fifteenth century of a widespread cult of Saint Catherine in County Donegal and Killybegs are not invalidated by the foregoing. That is to say there is no doubt there was indeed some knowledge there of this popular saint prior to 1515. More especially it must that have been the case amongst those who had gone on pilgrimage to Lough Derg even before the establishment of the cult at Killybeg's Holy Well. In the fifteenth century there was a growing antipathy to pilgrimages (especially those presenting visions or miracles purporting to assist a canonisation process rather than for penance.) There was much hesitancy about the cave at Lough Derg where penitents could supposedly undergo the actual tortures of Purgatory applied by real demons yet surviving to tell the tale.When the canon of Eymstadt failed to receive these experiences and noted there were others who had paid considerable sums to obtain them, he complained to Rome. Could it be that Saint Catherine had a case at Rome for canonisation at that time?

The heavenly voice heard at Saint Catherine's martyrdom offered penances during life for expiation of sin. This was interpreted as meaning that penances would suffice instead of requiring a Purgatory after death. Severe penitential practises must have been offered for those coming to Lough Derg afterwards in order to receive for the site its new recognition. Taken as an alternative to the supposed pre-death Purgatory formerly offered, this apparently fell well with the theology of Purgatory and indulgences being developed in Rome in the fifteenth century and declared at the Council of Trent in the sixteenth.

As Townlands
(a) "Saint Catherine's" or "Rosdagamph" near Enniskillen. Lisgoole, originally a house of Augustinian, canon's regular according to **Peadar Livingstone** in his *The Fermanagh Story* (1969) p.44 (It was later Franciscan). Now ruined, it lies not far away. There was an important scriptorium at Liscoole in days gone by. Since there is no doubt these canon's were Arroashian it must now be concluded some of them also followed Saint Catherine for a time.

(b) Kilcatherina in County Westmeath is near an early Irish monastic site (Kilcrumper) No account of its late medieval history has been found. Like the similarly named Kilcatherina in Kerry Diocese (See p.14) a native saint may be hidden
by   way of a substitution of 'Catherine'. See also **Bradley** *Kilkenny* (1988 p.11)

(c) Rincarren in Cork Diocese (Also 'Charles Fort') is also the name of a former parish. The parish evolved around a notable church 'Teampall na Trionoide'. At one time Saint Catherine's Abbey, Waterford was impropriate of it. The Church of Ireland church is today dedicated to Saint Catherine.[134] The name may be an englishing of "Rinn Chatherine"a possible gaelic form.

(d) Kathleen's Falls, the site of the Hydrogeneration Station on River Erne (Ballyshannon) seems to be called after Ceithlen, the founder of Enniskillen, wife of Balor the Fomorian Chief.

---

[134] See **Bolster** (1972) (already cited) pp 264-.266 Also **Brandon** (1971) (already cited)

**Figure No 20 Saint Duilech's Church, Balgriffin, Co. Dublin
Photographed by D. Welch of Strabane (Ca 1900)**

As Holy Wells.

(a) A Holy Well situated at Conwal, Letterkenny, County Donegal, Diocese of Raphoe

This Holy Well site is beside the spot where the defeated Irish officers from a Cromwelliann battle site (Scarriffhollis) were executed.(1650) The well is dedicated to Saint Catherine.[135] It is no longer frequented and no stations have been held there for many years. It is a suspect repetition of the Killybegs saint; brought to the site following the massacre. (Perhaps it was Saint Fiacre, patron of Conwal Parish, who was substituted for since he had not intervened in some way over the terrible decimation of the flower of the Irish resistance to Cromwell. He is still remembered at the spot as his reputed tomb is nearby)[136]

(b) At Tullow, County Carlow.

Besides those mentioned earlier there is one, which appears somewhat out of place, unless Tullow Priory was Victorine,a fact which is not known — **Gwynn and Hadcock** simply list it under "Augustinian Canons". Edward O'Toole [137] describes it as at Castlemore, Tullow, County Carlow, situated near the then home of the Eustace family. The Holy Well was restored by a member of this family in 1870 according to an inscription at it that mentions "St. Kathleen." Beside the Eustace former home, near NewAbbey Kilcullen County Kildare, there is also a reputed effigy of Saint Catherine. (See **Hunt**: Plate 216)

(c) Catherine's Well, Abbeyside, Dungarvan, County Waterford

Here there is a former 'Catherine's Well' the location of which seems too near the parish Church of Abbeyside, an ancient site, not to be of significance. It is shown on O.S. Maps, of various dates, with and without the appellation 'St.'[138] But the Well has long since disappeared. There are ruins attached to the Parish Church where was once the O.S.A. friary of Dun na Mainistreach. The foundations of the "Old Friary" have been identified as those of a still older church,[139] perhaps once the church of the Keynsham Abbey 'Farm' referred to in **White**.[140] Keynsham Abbey's property in the diocese of Limerick's had advowsons there too. The abbey is recorded as having been given to the church of Dungarvan by Thomas, Earl of Desmond in 1415. This surely must be where the 'Abbey Farm' was located. (See footnote No. 72)

---

[135] See **Henry Morris** *The Holy Wells of Donegal* in *Bealoideas* 1939
[136] According to Maire MacNeill such supplanting is not unusual where a native saint has not proved his efficacy. (See p 129 of her book where she tells of Saint Bernard supplanting Saint Patrick after a plague.)
[137] In *Bealoideas 1933*
[138] See Arial Survey of Dungarvan including Abbeyside at page 115 (The first edition O.S. Map 1848 has the word `St)
[139] See **Rev. Thomas C. Butler's** *Journey of an Abbey* (Dublin 1973). There is a good photograph at p 163 of **Michael Moore's** *Archaeological Inventory, of County Waterford* (Dublin 1999). See also **William Fraher's** booklet *The Augustinians in Abbeyside* (Dungarvan 1990)
[140] **N.B.White** (1943) p. 352 mentions a considerable Farm, valued at 40.1i,at the Dissolution. It may be possible to guess its boundary from descriptions of adjoining burgaries given in the *Civil Survey* of 1657. (**Simington** Ed. Dublin1937) An attempt at this has been made at this with the help of a map issued with the Report on the formation of Municipal Towns in 1825.

(d) Holy Well at Killybegs, County Donegal.

The small ruined Friary here (see Figure No 16.) is within a short distance of the Holy Well dedicated to Saint Catherine. The Friary site is traditionally the one where the Celtic monks set up their monastic settlement with their cloghaun cells, or 'cealla beaga'; (i.e. 'the little huts') thus the name 'Killybegs' From the air the enclosure may be seen to conform with the ring shape of early religious settlements known from elsewhere.[141]

When the friars came, in mid sixteenth century (under the auspices of Toirdealbhach Mac Suibhne as outlined above) typically they made full use of whatever they found abandoned. Originally, the natural spring (the old monks' source of water for domestic purposes) would by degrees inevitably have transferred a sense of their holiness to it. If curative properties were sometimes reported for the waters, as would be natural, the spring became a Holy Well dedicated to some early missionary monk possibly St. Ciaran of Saidhir who had visited the area. (See footnote 108)

It may have been, as just said,originally under another saint's name, but with the arrival of Máire Ni Mháille's friars, Saint Catherine became substituted for it in the manner outlined earlier(Chapter 2 p.26). Such was the way Christianity often made progress over the early centuries. That it happened here at the time when the pious Máire introduced her personal patron (with the combined agency - if unwitting-of the Franciscan Friars) should occasion little doubt.[142]

A pilgrimage/Pattern was long connected with the Killybegs Holy Well (Known in the folklore as 'Turas na gCeall' 'The pilgrimage of the huts'). The lengthy procession and prayers at an uncertain time of year (for weather) may have been a deterrent to its continuing outdoors. In recent years it is often held indoors.

---

[141] Illustrations are hard to find. See one on aerial photograph of 'Cashel with remains of cloghaun huts' in **E.R.Norman and J-K.S St. Joseph** *(Eds) The Early Development of Irish Society(* Cambridge. 1969) particularly No - 28 "Cashel near Kilmalkadar Co. Kerry"

[142] See **Chartles Conaghan's** *History and Antiquities of Killybegs* (1974)pp 114 and 151 -153 for a discussion re whether the Friary was either Franciscan or Dominican. Conaghan gives reasons for believing the Order present was Dominican and not Third Order Franciscan, because of the interest taken by the Dominicans in the canditature of Quentin O'Higgins O.P. for the bishopric of Raphoe. This was blocked by Chief Aodh Dubh O'Domhnaill. O'Higgins was thought to have been Rector of Killybegs for a time (though some think he only preached a mission there). In any case he was called back to Sligo for important work at Rome (dates inconclusive) (See **Rev.Thomas F. Flynn's** *The Irish Dominicans* (1993) p. 42-43). Information on O' Higgins is contradictory. **Aubrey Gwynn** in *his Province of Armagh* says he was Franciscan and never Rector of Raphoe or elected Bishop of Raphoe. In **Fr. P O Gallchoir's** review of **Conaghan** (1974) *in Donegal Annual* (1975-76) p.212 He agrees with the author that it was possibly a Dominican who introduced the patronage of Saint Catherine but thinks not O'Higgins. **Flynn** however gives his date of death as 1548.; **Gwynn** as 1539. It is clear there were two "Con O'Higgins "in the record. The evidence, such as it is, does not favour a Dominican as founder of the cult in Killybegs. **C.P Meehan** *(The Franciscan Monasteries in the 17th Century (1877)* seems to have had records of a provincial of the Franciscan Order (Mooney) dated no later than 1616 mentioning Killybegs as one of their (former) Third Order houses devoted to education (The 'native princes 'taking special care to settle large endowments towards the education of their people'')

Effigies and others

Including those mentioned earlier, **John Hunt** (Dublin and London 1974) has listed many of the stone carved effigies of Saint Catherine of Alexandria which he found in Ireland as follows in his book where he supplied illustrations in Volume 2 (Plates). These sculptured effigies occur at Howth, County Dublin. (Plate192), Castlemartin, Count Kildare. (Plate 208), Callan, County Kilkenny (Plate 321 reproduced at Figure No.16 above), New Abbey, Kilcullen, County Kildare (Plate 216). Two at Jerpoint Abbey, County Kilkenny (Plate 294) (See also Figure No. 7 herein for photograph of one of these. provided courtesy of Dúchas The Heritage Council), Two at Saint Canice's Cathedral, Kilkenny (Plates 311 and 318), at Askeaton. County. Limerick (Plate 269), Castletown, County Meath, Duleek, County. Meath (Plate 199), Dunsany, County Meath, Sligo, County Sligo (Plate 268 of the O Criain Tomb). Rock of Cashel, County. Tipperary (Plate 324), Lismore Cathedral, County Waterford (Plate 337) (See also Figure No. 17 above). At Mothel County Waterford (Plate 335) and at Waterford The Rice Tomb (Plate 273)

Some of these have received detailed scholarly treatment individually.[143] **Hunt** himself remarked on the importance and popularity of the subjects of his study p.146 stating "apart from the Apostles the saint with the greatest number of existing representations is Saint Catherine of Alexandria"[144]

---

[143] See, for example, **J.R. Garstin's** well-illustrated *"On the McCragh Tomb in Lismore Cathedral"* in JRSAI Pt 4 (1904). **Geoffrey Hand** in his *History of Irish Catholicism* III
(The Church in the English Lordship p 35): remarks "Art can be a helpful guide to devotion. The frequent occurrence of figures of Saint Catherine of Alexandria on altar tombs in the Lordship, for example, shows how the Anglo-Normans brought her cult with them". His remarks in the continuing paragraph are also useful.

[144] See **John Hunt** (1974) already cited p 109. **Hunt** seems not to have adverted to the sculptures at Saint Catherine de O'Conyl, illustrated by **Dianne Hall** (2003) (already cited) or another at the Black Abbey, Kilkenny, both of Saint Catherine. The former should be compared with **Hunt** Plate 26, Cat 23 p231

Figure No.21 Saint Catherine with Saints Patrick and Mochuda
on the McGrath Tomb, Lismore Cathedral

Figure No.22 Ruins of Augustinian Priory (Victorine) at Newtown-Trim, Co. Meath

Others

Chantry Altars Though a few altars for other saints have been noted, only three in Ireland for Saint Catherine are known to the present writer. (i) One is at Saint James' church in Cork City. This is mentioned by Evelyn Bolster (1972) as receiving a bequest under the Wychendon will. (ii) **Colm Lennon**[145] explains about another that it was of the Guild of Saint Katherine in Saint David's Church, Naas, County Kildare. The burgesses of the town provided this altar at this time with altar-priests. Under the Henrician suppression this altar "of The Fraternity of Saint Katherine, Naas", was dissolved. It was the property of Saint' John's Hospital, "An Augustinian house." (iii) **H.F. Berry**,[146] quoting Ware's Antiquities, mentions a cell appropriate to the canons of Saint Victor of Saint Thomas' Abbey, Dublin, at or near Enniscorthy, which was dedicated to "St. John the Evangelist". According to **Moore's** Inventory, the remains, such as they may be, "are not visible at ground level." The attachment to Saint Thomas' abbey apparently took place in the late thirteenth century. According to **Gwynn and Hadcock** a charter of ca. 1230 "reserved to the canons the chapel of St Katherine." It probably had a chantry altar. (The site had originally been a native Irish monastic settlement of Saint Senan.) It is mentioned in **Samuel Lewis Dictionary** (1837) cofirming Ware's account. St Senan was an early bishop of Ferns.

---

[145] **Newport White** (1943) p 155.

[146] **H.F.Berry's** '*Signs*' in JRSAI (1892) p 107ff

Map No IV. Aerial Survey of Dungarvan including (Abbeyside) showing the relationship of 'Catherine's Well' to the Old (fifthteenth century) O.S.A.Abbey on the same site. The A.S. has been compared with Waterford 6 inch to one mile O.S. Map No 13 (The A.S.is by permission of Ordnance Survey Ireland, Permit No MP006804 Ordnance Survey Ireland /Government of Ireland) - The 1843 Edition of 6 inch scale map has 'St. Catherine's Well'

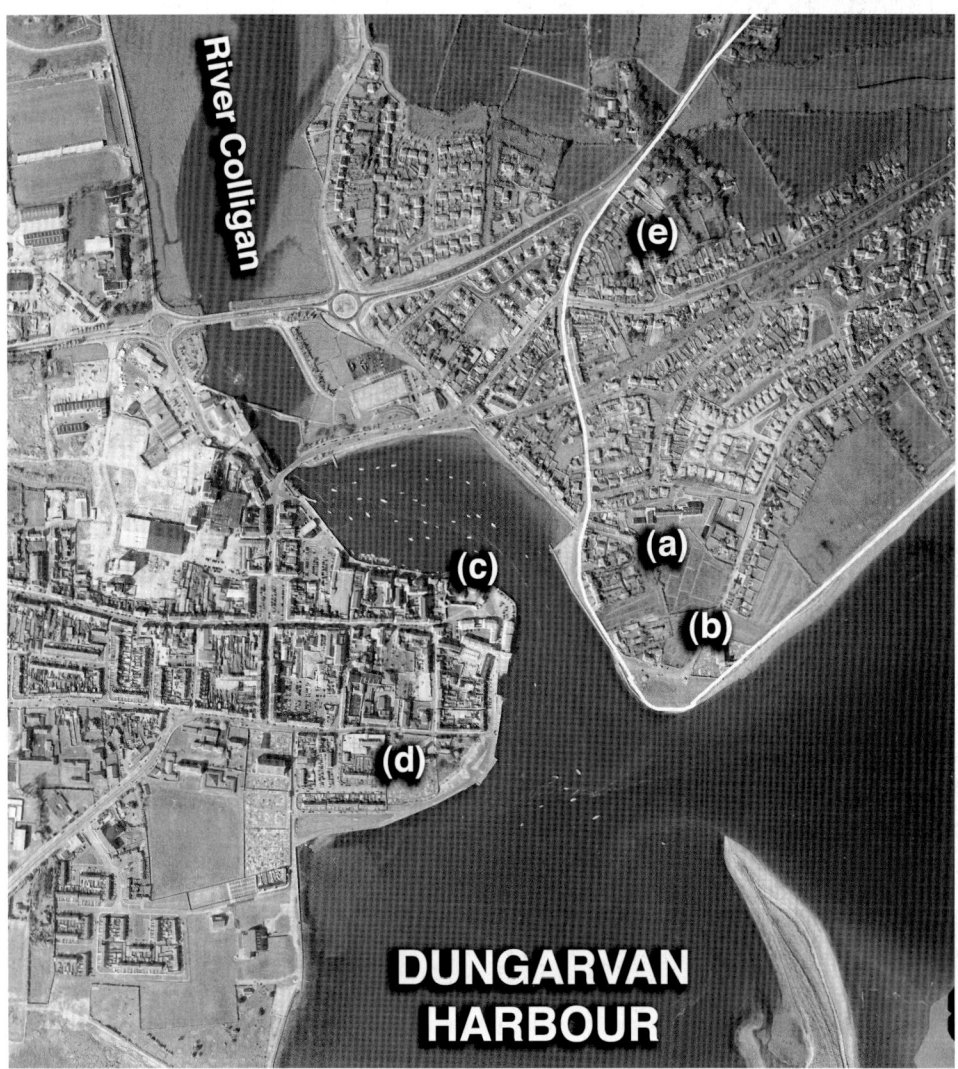

(a)   Site of Catherine Holy Well (Closed in)
(b)   Ruins of O.S.A Friary on foundations of early Canons Regular House
(c)   Dungarvan Castle (seat) of Earls of Desmond, Lords of Decies (c.1400)
(d)   St. Mary's Church (C.O.I.) (pre-invasion wall of church ruin)
(e)   Conjectural boundary of farm of the Somerset Canons

Figure No.22a
Stained Glass window
Duncannon Church, Co. Wexford

Figure No.22b
Stained Glass window
Killybegs Church, Co. Donegal

CHAPTER. 17

May there not be true history at the core of some folklore?

In countries such as Ireland of the fifth century onwards, when conversion from paganism had only relatively recently taken place, the Christian Church raised little objection to the reappearance of a former (i.e.pagan) religious system, so long as it was reinterpreted in terms of the new Christianity. The acceptance in Ireland of some things questionably heathenish, such as practices associated with Crom Cruaic (see Chapter 13) would have been execrated by the newly arriving Anglo-Norman clerics of a critical disposition especially those settling in the Pale.

These men had, of course, the experience of dealing with similar situations before leaving England. It has been suggested earlier that the cult of Saint Catherine may have been permitted in Ireland successfully to replace earlier cults of doubtful antecedents at a few sites. Irish saints, indeed became the new patrons of certain Holy Wells[147] of undoubted former pagan provenance.[148] This was undoubtedly was known to the incomers. The Lammas rites of Crom Cruaic would certainly also be disapproved of by those coming from England and Wales. Some of his sites in Ireland would, of course in addition have ethnic symbolism. Many Holy Wells following the conquest must have retained a separate ethnic character through showing their non-Britishness and anyway displaying the Irish 'barbaric' character. In many cases this would gradually diminish with time. Later, after the Reformation, and remaining Irishness could be quietly ignored. Especially in districts which did not cease taking their religion from Rome, ethnic nationalistic displays of religion became absorbed in a 'vulgar' system of penitential 'rounds',supposedly an adaptation of ancient ('pagan') rituals, for the purpose of doing honour to Irish saints.These practises becamestandardised for many shrines for Irish saints and, in the remoter areas, even for Saint Catherine. The annual Lammas pilgrimage to the site in County Mayo where Saint Patrick's great success story on the Croagh (where he had ejected Crom Cruaic from his mountain fastness) is particularly relevant to the argument which follows.

---

[147] Elaborated by **Delahaye** (1955) in his chapter *Pagan Memories and Survivals*

[148] See **Anne Ross's** *Pagan Celtic Britain* (London 1967)pp 22-31

The 'penitential' practices "Patterns" performed at many important Irish saints' sites were tolerated by Roman Catholic clergy for a long time, though with some reluctance, especially when those attending at some sites became boisterous or normal religious practice (attendance at church or mass was neglected). If there was a delay in their condemnation it may have been due to a reluctance to proceed against something so distinctively Irish. The similar reluctance to condemn the debilitating 'Prophesies of Saint Columbkille' has been discussed **by E. O'Curry.** in his *'Manners and Customs of the Ancient Irish'*

The Legends of Tailtiu Revisited

The wider area of Teltown, if the suggestion of **Maire MacNeill** be accepted, was the site in late medieval times of a relapsed semi - pagan shrine devoted to Crom Cruaic. It was probably one of those sites of the Pale felt most objectionable by the arriving Anglo-Norman ecclesiastics in the thirteenth century. To bring folklore studies to bear on the matter, one must look to **Maire MacNeill** for guidance. She makesvery pertinent information available in her *The Festival of Lughnasa*.[149] According to the *Tripartite Life of Saint Patrick* he founded a church at Donoghpatrick he is not credited with. Averting to the Teltown House- site about mile away which is surprising. This is now posited (above Chapter X) as having been the centre site of the pagan Aonach Tailteann. Though there is an account of the Donaghpatrick site there is no specific reference to this centre shrine (Telltown) being converted from its presumed paganism until the Anglo-Normans arrived and built a church there.[150] Legendary accounts of a former shrine there (as in *Tain Bo Cuailgne, Yellow Book of Lecan* etc.) refer to implicitly pagan 'Games' taking place at the ancient graves. After Saint Patrick's late representatives from Armagh (as demonstrated in the Tripartite Life) had passed along, the 'Games' were deemed semi-Christian at worst[151] At any rate the Teltown site was ignored.

---

[149] *Festival* p.315 The Anglo-Nomans overran County Meath as far as "Kill-Teltain" in 1170, (AFM.) Thereafter, Kilteltan ('The Church at Teltown') for a. long time was noted to be a point establishing the boundary of the Pale. (It may be assumed there had not been a church there before that.) NB. The circling of the site with St. Erc's bones in 895.
[150] **Henry Morris** in an article *Where was Aonach Tailteann?* (JRSAI 1930 Pt.11) proposed the megalithic site of Sliabh na Caillighe (Loughcrew) as the original Aonach Tailteann site. Based on readings from *The Tain*, the theory has not gained general acceptance.
[151] **MacNeill** (*Festival* p.320) Also see **Kathleen Hughes'** *Early Christian Ireland* (N.Y.1972) p232n

Until the ethnic Irish population had all but left the area and what remained of the old rituals just mentioned had moved to Martry just a mile away across the River Blackwater, the games/assembly site probably remained intact. (or so **MacNeill** seems to think but without all its pagan connotations). Little will be known about the questions implied until the Teltown site is archaeologically examined and the antiquity of the graves settled. 'Saint Patrick' must have known of the strong residue of pagan sanctity at Teltown. A boundary, between tuatha evidently passed between Donoughpatrick and Teltown; perhaps one sept converted while the other did not. What may be inferred though, from a combination of folklore and the factual presence of an early church at Teltown, is that upon the arrival of the Anglo-Normans, Crom Dubh (equivalent to 'Crom Cruaic',the male Lughnasa entity), was driven out along the road ('Crom Dubh's Road') which runs by Teltown – as posited so convincingly by **Maire MacNeill**[152] Also she makes — though rather obliquely—the suggestion that Saint Catherine of Teltown perhaps became identified with the Caoranach, the female Lughnasa entity she often refers to. If so, could it not be that Catherine was substituted for her in a late effort at blessing the site? Even if assumed that the Victorine canons from Kells were the final agents of the conversion, it would not be beyond their imaginative capacity to do so especially if they had come to it rather late, in the fifteenth century.

MacNeill sets out several folklore accounts of Saint Patrick dealing with the Caoranach, one of them at Lough Derg in County Donegal. At Lough Derg there is evident substitution involved. The reader will recall the note (At pages 110 above) concerning an early 'bed' in Saint Catherine's honour at the pilgrimage site. We perhaps see in these ancient stories the residue of a widespread legend of the "Driving out of Lugh" (Teltown) and elsewhere; together with a traditional belief of an ejection at first attempted by early missionary monks but completed by the Anglo- Normans. If Saint Catherine was substituted as a beneficial entity to replace the expelled malign Caoranach, one may see how folklore has provided a ready explanation for medieval Christian devotions still surviving in her honour at the Parish of Oristown.

---

[152] See **MacNeill** *Festival* (*Dublin* 1962, reprinted 1992) For the Caorthanach at Lough Derg, another Catherine site, see the same pp 50-53 and 58 also pp 525, 530)

A suggested factual (historical) amalgam of folklore's of Saint Catherine at Killybegs and Ventry.

Killybegs 2

A plausible suggestion has been made by Spanish visitors to Killybegs recently in relation to the folklore of Saint Catherine's Holy Well as provided by Canon Maguire. Its interest for them derived from the saint's popularity in Spain in the sixteenth century and later. There she is known as Santa Catalina (in the Catalan language 'Santa Catarena'). For most Spaniards it is quite disappointing that she played such a poor part in permitting the destruction of the Spanish Armada in 1588. That a Bishop from a distressed ship had blessed the Killybegs Holy Well and "named it after Saint Catherine" before departing thy found of great interest. They wondered if the bishop was from the *La Girona* which is known to have sought shelter at Killybegs harbour. The Holy Well as we have seen above, was dedicated to Saint Catherine of Alexandria perhaps half a century before. To have become aware of this astonishing fact (unknown to them as having a full historical basis) would have intrigued the crews attending the blessing.

La Girona was one of the many ships commandeered by the King of Spain from Mediterranean ports for the Armada. It was a galliasse, not at all built for the hazardous Atlantic. The crew, too, may have been. largely drawn from their home province of Catalonia some even from the eponymous town of Girona. The town is not far from the sea and traditionally supplied sailors and oarsmen to the many ports lying between Palamos and Barcelona. The ship belonged to the Naples squadron of the Armada which sailed out of Spain into a great disaster (but for Queen Elizabeth and all England — confirmation that God was with her/ them).

That there were clerical passengers on board the vessel *La Girona* which struggled into Killybegs after the disaster, is very probable. **Fallon** in his *The Armada in Ireland*, states that rosters from the time, which have been examined in Spain, show that the bishop of Killaloe known as "Enrique Brenne" (Brennan) was present at departure of this ship. Another (the same?) Irish bishop is mentioned as a survivor in **Evelyn Hardy's** *Survivors of the Armada* (although not listed amongst the dead of the *La Girona*[153]). High level clerics even Spanish bishops would have been provided on the ships to look after the injured and their immortal souls. There was bound to be at least one bishop amongst the crew who made their way to Killybegs from the several ships which came to grief along the Donegal coast.

---

[153] **Niall Fallon** in his *The Armada in Ireland* (London 1978) gives the bishop of Killaloe as going down with *La Gerona* (*p.221)*

Canon Maguire(page 124 below) learned from the tradition adhering to the Holy Well of Killybegs that Saint Catherine's patronage came from the time of the early 'Little Huts'— and a very doubtful foundation of the fifteenth century friary at Ballinasaggat we accept this? It must now be rejected in favour of the proposition that it began with the Third Order friary or again, it may be said when the Armada ships left Lisbon on their fateful voyage in 1588. (A fifteenth century Hospital dedicated to Santa Catarina at the town of Girona ensured she would have been a familiar saint to many of the crew of the *La Girona*.)

The *La Girona,* after refitting, at Killybegs, in the best fashion the ships' complement could achieve, again set sail from Killybegs in October 1588, this time heavily laden with valuables, munitions and additional personnel collected from several other Armada ships which had foundered in the locality. If the ship's bishop were to go to the Holy Well to pray for a successful voyage home, it was only natural that he should. His visit, however, left a lasting impression on the native people of Killybegs. Because of their ship's condition and the lack of victuals (or rather, it seems, for barrels to keep them fresh in) the Captain decided, rather than running directly across the Bay of Biscay for home, to make for Scotland. Unfortunately the *La Girona* struck the rocks at night off Fair Head, Co. Antrim with the loss of over 1400 lives. Earlier in the same disastrous year the large merchantman the *Santa Catalina*, laden down with marines, was unable to avail of the power of her ships patron as was expected of her when she sank opposite Plymouth after colliding with another Armada ship.[154] The business of war does not seem to be within her patronage.

---

[154] See **Garret Mattingly's** *The Defeat of the Spanish Armada* (London 1959) p 394

Ventry 2

La Girona was only one of the many ships of the Armada which came to grief off the coast of Ireland. Our knowledge of two others in particular gives us reason for pause since their story enables a rationalisation to be made of what seems a garbled story of Saint Catherine at Ventry, Co Kerry. One is drawn to the information recently garnered by the sub-aqua archaeological investigation of the ships *Santa Maria de la Rosa* and *San Juan* both of which sank in the Blaskets Sound just four miles from Ventry Harbour.

The story which has come down to us of the origin of Saint Catherine's cult at Ventry conveys more than a hint of a survivor from a ship clinging to a barrel and reaching Ventry beach. Indeed it is of the nature of folklore that it often offers a credible basis for undistinguished stories. This one is strongly indicated as also deriving from the time of the Armada wrecks. The folklore of Saint Catherine at Ventry appears a near approximation to a true account of an Armada survivor succeeding in coming ashore and conveying to some pious local persons his gratitude to Santa Catarina for his safety.[155] The Sovereign at Dingle Port, James Trant, was Anglo-Irish. The unfortunate survivor would have had little chance of avoiding summary execution as an Armada survivor either from him or from the terrible Sir Edward Denny from Tralee, but not however before transmitting his devotion to his own patron saint. Thus strengthening the existing devotion already amongst his those who had brought him ashore.

---

[155] Nothing in these remarks is intended to suggest that there was not already in 1588 a flourishing cult of Saint Catherine of Alexandria (Naomh Catariona) in the district of Ventry as at Killybegs. **Miss Hickson** had noted the Deaneries of Aghadoe and Ardfert and worked out with others their connection to Saint Catrerine's Abbey, Waterford and the Taxation of 1300 (JRSAI 1889 p.114)

Some Conclusions

This survey does not offer any more than a little perceived local history of several places appertaining to the cult of Saint Catherine of Alexandria in Ireland. A much neglected area, it seemed to this writer to be calling for scholarly investigation. Historical authenticity of some of the accounts given here may be questioned, certain jumps of dubious logic being perhaps, easily detectable. Attention is drawn., however, to a fact not easy of rebuttal i.e. that the incoming Anglo-Normans took certain advantage, from being of the same religious persuasion as the Irish, but used this in a lamentable fashion. Excusable perhaps for daughty invaders attempting to gain ascendancy over the lands, trade, property and all other aspects of a 'barbaric' people who appeared, except from time to time when over pressed., rather easy to make subject to them perhaps more honourably if they were only to have had a little patience. (The standard histories appear to concentrate on occasions of armed resistance to obvious cases of injustice) Coming as they did from a powerful Norman Empire the incomers were able to influence matters at Rome.

Opportunities which presented themselves in the religious sphere were taken forward there immediately or with the least delay. Such matters as lobbying of the Papal Court, controlling the appointments of bishops, restricting the return of temporalities to native appointees, putting forward the pretence of being the official representatives of the Lateran Council,[156] and insisting on the fealty of bishops to the crown are evident examples of this. While these had important consequences other lessor activities were quite insidious.

Take for example the imposition of relatives of the Anglo-Norman magnates upon the monasteries as superiors while excluding at the same time the Irish from noviceships. This was cunning. Excusable perhaps for the new religious houses they themselves established, but such a policy applied to the old houses could only be in anticipation of an eventual complete take - over. The advancement of the cult of Saint Catherine did not need to be pressed. Its attractions were agreeable to the religion of the native people. The native chieftains were hardly aware of the nature of the undermining taking place of their ancient rights and culture by religious means and by other associated creeping stratagems.

---

[156] See paragraph "Church, Religion, Literacy and Learning" in **David Carpenter's** *The Struggle for Mastery* (London 2001)

Figure No.23a
Figure Sculpture of Saint Catherine of
Alexandria, The Black Church,
Kilkenny

Figure No.23b
Alebaster Figure of Saint Catherine
of Alexandria at
Granary Museum, Waterford

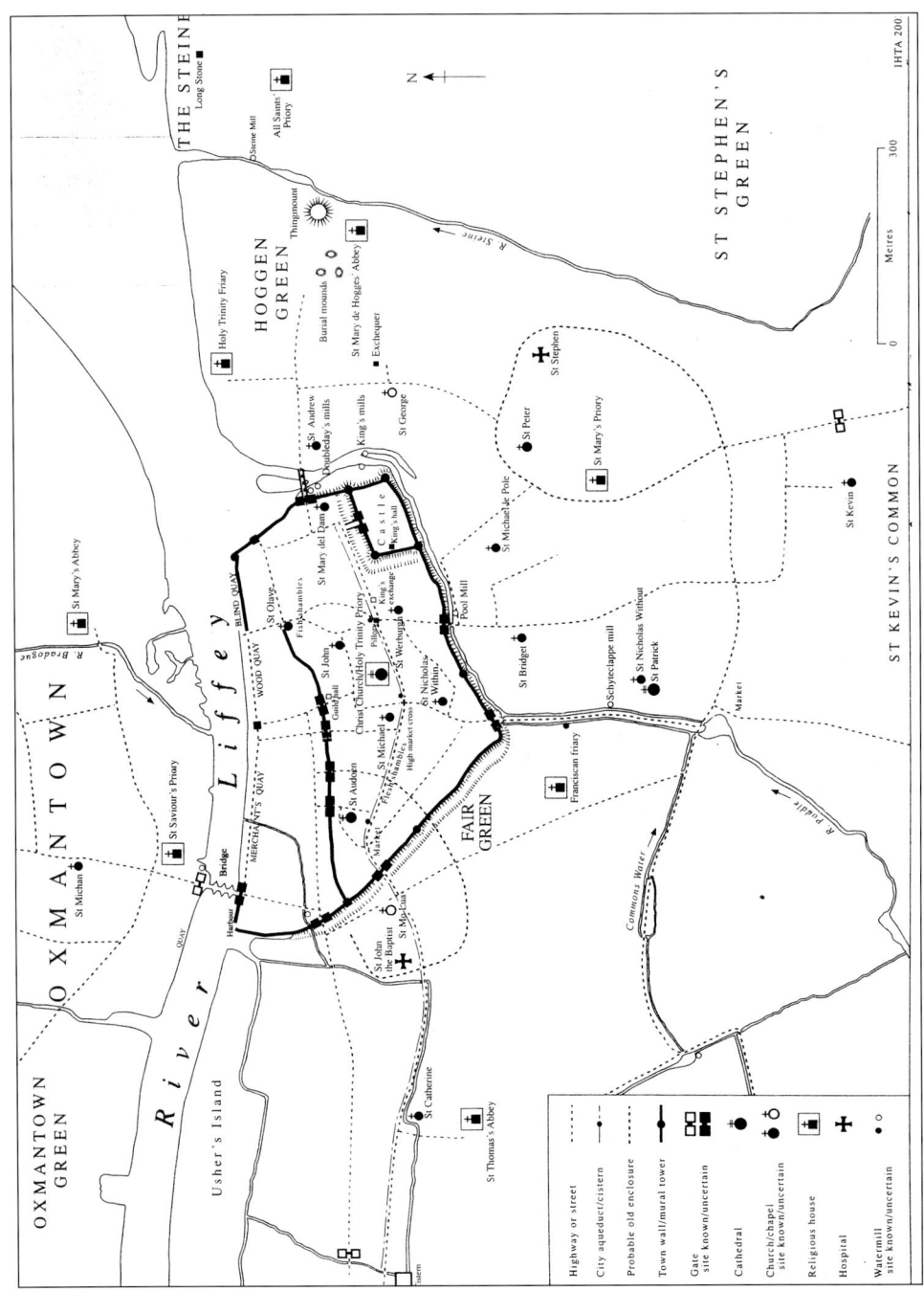

Map Of Dublin ca. 1300
Taken from Dublin Part I of Irish Historie Towns Atlas No 14 (1610)
by **H.B. Clarke**.(Royal Irish Academy, Dublin 2002)
Reproduced with kind permission of the Academy.

Appendix 1 (Extract from Canon Maguire's History)

Chapter IV Parish of Killybegs and Killaghtee

The origin and position of the "Little Churches" from which the parish derives its name, are nowhere explained in ecclesiastical, history, or in biographies of our saints. Tradition represents the village as dedicated to St. Catharine, as its patron from the sixth century, when the "little churches," or early monastic "cells," were first erected on its peaceful banks. The details of the story are interesting, even if they present a seemingly fabulous and well-worn surface. "A ship once arrived here from unknown parts: among the passengers was a saintly bishop, who conducted the party and crew to a nook on the neighbouring hillside to offer a prayer of thanksgiving. He blessed the since famous well, dedicated it to Catharine of Egypt, is not Irish; it comes from the Greek word catharos, signifying pure, and in the days of SS. Conal, Cathair, Naul, and Mac Brackain, St. Catharine of the Wheel was venerated with singular devotion in many Continental and Irish seaports, including Cork and Dublin. Most probably it was foreign pilgrims who first introduced her name into the familiar invocation at Lough Derg. The fame of the saint for her astounding intellect and her heroic fortitude is quite a sufficient reason to account for the dedication of wells in her honour, both in this district and in other parts of Ireland, where she is specially venerated. Wells of St. Patrick, St. Columba, St. Naul, &c., are named after the patron of the place; and hence the explanation is superfluous, even if it appears plausible, that one of the forms of torture applied to St. Catharine was her immurement in a deep-dug pit, or closed "well." Certain it is that O'Malley was popularly regarded as the victim of St. Catharine's wrath in 1513, and that Mac Swine of Banagh had founded the Killybegs Monastery about half a century before, for the non-observant Franciscans, under the title of St. Catharine's. In 1837, the official report states: "No remains of the friary, but some ruins of the ancient Castle of St. Catharine yet exist" meaning Mac Swine's Castle, which stood on an elevation immediately adjoining the grounds of the monastery.

The exact location of the "little cells," erected cenobites, it is impossible to determine; nor can it be even conjectured with any show of probability whether these structures were of stone and of the bee-hive order, like those to be seen in Innismurry, or of clay and irregular shape, like those of Clonard or Raphoe. It is fairly probable that hey occupied the west bank of the creek, and that the same site was subsequently covered by the church and friary of the Tertiaries. The ruined oratory, still partially preserved, is believed to have been attached to the Bishop's manor, and the Franciscan chapel, which was retained for Catholic purposes down to 1809, forms the nave of the undamaged shell. The apse, on the south side was a later addition. Before Roger Jones commenced the building of a Protestant church within the Borough in 1617, the Planters had appointed St. Catharine's; and, even afterwards, buried their dead within its precincts.

Extract from **Canon** *E. Maguire's History of the Diocese of Raphoe,(Dublin 1920)* Chapter IV Parish of Killybegs and Killaghtee

Appendix 2

Facsimile of page 1 Beatha agus Bas Chaitreach Fína
(Máire Ní Mháille's Life of Saint Catherine of Alexandria
(See **Paul Walsh** (Ed.) *The Book of the MacSweeneys* and
Gearoid Mac Niocaill's account of it in *Eigse 8*

Appendix 3
Hymn to Saint Catherine "Maid of Alexandria"
by Donal Martin of Killybegs (2000) (by permission of the composer)

"MAID OF ALEXANDRIA"

Maid of Alexandria to you we humbly pray.
Keep us on the proper path; guide us on our way.
Saint Catherine who brought the sailor safely
through the foam
Lead us also in your care to our heavenly home.

Virgin of that ancient land, martyr for your cause
You defied the might of Rome; scorned its cruel laws.
St. Catherine teach us all to stand for what is right.
In the hour of doubt and fear be our guiding light.

Many times they tortured you; tried to steal your pride.
Even in your darkest hour God was at your side.
So help us all St Catherine when we need your aid.
Give us strength to be like you, pure and fearless maid.

Appendix 3
Hymn to Saint Catherine "Maid of Alexandria"
by Donal Martin of Killybegs (2000) (by permission of the composer)

Appendix 5

The Legend of St. Catherine of Alexandria

by Ellen Fitzsimon (born O'Connell)

INTRODUCTION

Beneath Saint Clement's venerated dome,
Most perfect of the Basilicas of Rome,
(Where a good Irish friar hath done more
Than all the rich and pious had before
In many centuries), there met my sight
A fresco painting, not long given to light,
The which a noble, simple story told
Of triumph by Saint Catherine won of old
Against the heathen sages, and the day
When for the Christian Faith she gave her life away.
Recalling this and many a glorious feat
Of that great Saint, her legend I repeat,
Laying my homage humbly at her feet.

THE LEGEND

In Alexandria, centuries ago,
Amid a circle of philosophers,
Of solemn sages, throughout Egypt famed,
With others from the walls of palmy Rome,
And Greece's classic clime, sate Catherine,
A Christian virgin, stately, fair, and young,
Descended of a high Imperial race,
And further graced with genius' golden gifts.
Calmy she sate, and disputation held
With all those mighty masters of the mind,
Alike on sciences and curious arts,
On all thy varied forms, Philosophy!
And higher still, Theology divine.
In admiration, mixed with awe, the crowd
Of listeners hung upon her silvery tones,
The while with wondrous eloquence she spake
The might, the majesty of Heaven's ways
Revealed to men! refuting thoroughly
All arguments, however plausible,
By her opponents brought forth to support
The worn-out faith on fable solely founded,
On fable, feeble, foolish, and unclean!

At length the pseudo-sages – struggling still
Against conviction, nor content to own
Defeat, except by silence – suddenly
Broke up the assembly, on some poor pretence,
And each departed, feeling envious hate
Invade his inmost soul 'gainst Catherine,
Who thus had humbled them before the people.
She sought her secret cell, to purity,
To constant faith, true love, and hope divine,
Kept sacred. There, before the crucifix
Kneeling, she cried, "To Thee, to Thee, O Lord,
The glory and the praise that thou hast lent
Thy handmaid power to triumph in Thy name!"
Not many days now passed, ere to the city
Came Maximin; the tyrant Emperor.
Soon summoned to his court were all the nobles,
And all the brave, the youthful and the fair;
Amongst them Catherine, as a kinswoman
Of the Imperial Caeser, held high place
No less than for her bearing and her genius.
Scarce had the Emperor beheld the maid
When love (as fierce as hate) possessed his soul!
Oh, no! not love, but passion, such as fills
The brindled panther's panting breast for her
His bright-eyed, cruel co-mate of the woods!
All unaccustomed, save to swift success,
He signified his feelings, doubting not
Of joyful acceptation , Catherine,
Without or exultation or disdain,
Declined his suit. Fired by repulse,
He, who at first had nothing meant in honour,
Now cried, "Thou surely dost not understand
That Caeser woos thee for his bride, his Empress?"
Still calm, unmoved, the maid rejected him;
For she had bound herself by secret vow
The bride of Heaven alone, nor would resign
For earthly throne the virgin's privilege
To follow in the path the Lamb doth tread.
Foaming with fury, yet not daring aught
Against a daughter of Imperial line,
The tyrant saw her leave his courtly halls,
The while he cried, "Oh! for a safe revenge
On this insulting woman!"
           Since this earth
First ran its destined course around the sun,
Was never wanting to a tyrant's rage
Fit instrument! A false philosopher,
Of those whom Catherine lately overcame,
Gladly embraced the occasion offered him
To work her evil. To the infuriate Caesar

Did he denounce her as blasphemer 'gainst
The gods of Rome, of Athens, and of Eygpt,
As being that most vile of all vile things,
A Christian! Summoned to the dread tribunal
Of Maximin, who triumphed in the thought
Of humbling her, came now without delay
The lovely lady. Stately and serene
Did she approach, and, questioned of her faith,
Unhesitating owned herself a Christian.
The Emperor, his passion moved anew at sight
Both of her beauty and unflinching courage,
Offered her life and freedom on condition
That she unto the gods made sacrifice.
Again rejected, he went further still,
Promising safety, liberty of faith,
If she would only bless him with her hand.
Needs not to say what Catherine replied;
Enough that in his rage he sentenced her
Instant to perish by a fearful death,
By cruel torture on a whirling wheel!
His orders were obeyed. Amid the groans
Of many, and the secret tears of more,
The maid, upon whose brow sate peace and joy,
Was bound upon the wheel, while Maximin,
Panting for vengeance, loudly called upon
The executioner to do his duty.
The wretch approached to turn the fatal wheel,
To which the maiden was already bound,
When, lo! a miracle! As struck by lightening,
The horrid engine into pieces fell;
And Catherine, her arms crossed on her breast,
Stood, calmly there, uninjured and unbound!
Then rose up to the firmament a shout
Of jubilee from all the multitude,
"The gods forbid that Catherine should die!"
And breaking through the strongest barriers
They placed the virgin on a lofty car,
And drew her with rejoicing to her home!
The tyrant dared not then oppose the people
In their wild moment of enthusiasm;
But when dark night enwrapped the slumbering city,
Was Catherine seized, and secretly conveyed
To prison by his orders. There some days
She languished in the deepest of the dungeons.
Thence, still in silence and in secrecy,
Brought forth at dawn, she perished by sword,
Her latest breath breathed out in prayer and praise!
Towards morn, a rumour of the virgin's death
Spread through the city, whence derived none knew:
Nor did the people dare to speak aloud

Their doubts and fears upon the matter now;
For Maximin with armed satellites
Had filled each public square and market-place,
And made the craven hearted people quail
By vast display of force.
                              The night had come,
The dead of night. The city slumbering lay;
No star shone sparkling in the firmament,
But, like a pall, hung darkness on the earth:
When lo the sound such as no instrument,
No trumpet, save archangel's, e'er have out,
So sadly sweet, so thrilling, terrible,
Roused sudden from their sleep the citizens;
While, high in air, a dazzling, blinding light
Shone, 'neath whose glare the Pagan's all aghast,
Fell prone to earth, the while the Christians saw
A band of bright-wing'd angels cleave the sky,
Bearing the body of Saint Catherine,
And chanting hymns of triumph as they flew,
Until they reached the summit of a hill
Where they deposited their holy charge,
In safety on a spot where, long years after,
A church and monastery were up-raised,
Who owned Saint Catherine for their Patroness,
Their pious intercessor with the Lord!
Such is the legend handed down to us
In truth and wisdom from the ancient days.

Poem extracted from first issue of *The Irish Monthly* October 1873 pp204-207.

Figure 24 Stained Glass Window, Aughrim Church, Co. Galway

A SELECTION OF BOOKS REFERRED TO

Barrows J.A. and Brooks	St Wolfstan and his wolrd	Aldershot 2005
Ball, F. Elrington	A History of County Dublin	Dublin 1906
Begley, John	The Dioscese of Limerick, Ancient and Modern	Dublin 1906
Bolster, Evelyn	A History of the Diocese of Cork (Part I)	Shannon 1977
Bourke, Eamonn	Burke, People and Places	Whitegate,Co. Clare 2001
Bradley, John	Settlemen & Society in medieval Ireland	Kilkenny 1988
Bradshaw, Brendan	The Dissolution of the Religious Orders in Ireland under Henry VIII	Cambridge, 1974
Bradshaw, B, & Keogh D.(Eds.)	Christianity in Ireland - Revisiting the Story.	Blackrock 2002
Brandon,E.A	To Whom we Dedicated	Dublin 1971
Butler, Lionel et al-	Medieval Monasteries of Great Britain (Articles)	London 1983
Butler, Rev Thomas C. OSA	John''s Lane - A History of the Augustinian Friars in Dublin,	Dublin 1983
Canon D.L.	St Nicholas Bishop of Nyro	Ottawe 2002
Carpenter, David,	The Struggle for Mastery,	London 2003
Cartrwright, Jane	Celtic Hagiography and Saint's Cu l ts	Cardiff 2003
Conaghan, Charles,	History and Antiquities of Killybegs Parish.	Ballyshannon 1974
Rev. Patrick Corish (Ed.)	A History of Irish Catholicism (Parts 3 &4)	Dublin 1968
Cosgrove, Art,	Late Medieval Ireland (1370-1541)	Dublin 1981
Culleton, Edward.	Celtic and Early Christian Wexford	Dublin 1999
Cuppage, Judith.	Archaeological Survey of Corca Dhuibhne (Articles)	Ballyferriter 1986
Curtis, Edmund	A History of Medieval Ireland (1086-1513) 2nd Edition	London 1938
Gwynn,,Aubrey & Hadcock,R.N	Medieval Religious Houses (Ireland)	London 1970
De Breffny, Brian and Moran, James	The Churches and Abbeys of Ireland	London 1976
Delehaye, Hipppolyte	The Legends of the Saints (O'Loughlin's introduction)	Dublin 1998
Dickinson J. C.	The Origin of the Austin Canons and their Introduction into England	London 1950
Dolley, Michael	Anglo-Norman Ireland	Dublin 1972
Dunning, Robert	Somerset Monasteries	Stroud 2001
Duffy, Sean	Medieval Dublin (Parts 1 to 6)	Dublin 2000-5
Egan, Rev.Patrick CC	The Parish of Ballinasloe (Reprint)	Galway 1994
Frame, Robin	Ireland and Britain (1170-1450)	London 1988
Flanagan, Laurance	Ireland's Armada Legacy	Dublin 1998
Flannagan, Marie- Therese	Irish Society, Anglo-Norman Settlers and Angevin Kingship	Oxford 1993

Flynn, Thomas S.	The Irish Dominicans 1536 -1641	Blackrock 1998
Fallon, Niall	The Armada in Ireland	London, 1978
Gilbert John T.	Register of the Abbey, of St: Thomas the Martyr, Dublin	London 1889
Gwynn, Aubrey,Rev -SJ	The Irish Church, 11th and 12th Centuries	Blackrock 1992
Gwynn, Aubrey.Rev.S.J.	The Medieval Province of Armagh	Dundalk 1946
Harbison, Peter	Pilgrimage in Ireland	London 1991
Hardy, Evelyn	Survivors of the Armada	London 1966
Hall, Dianne	Women in the Church in Medieval Ireland ca.1140-1540	Dublin 2003
Haren,M.&De Pontfarcy, Y.	The Medieval Pilgrimage to St. Patrick' s Purgatory, Lough Derg	Enniskilllen 1988
Hayes McCoy, Gerard A	Scots Mercenary Forces in Ireland (1565 to 1603)	Dublin 1966 (reprint)
Head, Thomas (Ed.)	Medieval Hagiography, an Anthology	London 2001
Herity, Michael.(Ed.)	Ordnance Survey Letters-Meath	Dublin 2001
Jordan, W.C.	Europe in the High Midlle ages	London 2001
Lacy, Brian et al	Archaeological Survey of County Donegal	Lifford 1983
Lawrence, C, H.	Medieval Monasticism (3rd Ed.)	London 2001
Leask. Harold G.,	Irish Churches and Monastic Buildings	Dundalk 1955
Lefebre, Dom.,O.S.B.	Daily Missal (Articles)	Bruges
Lennon, Colm	Sixteenth Century Ireland: The Incomplete Conquest.	Dublin 1994
Lewis, Katherine J	The Cult of St.Katherine of Alexandria in late 'Medieval England	Woodbridge 2000
Lewis, Samuel	A Topographical Dictionary of Ireland.	London 1837
Livingstone, Peader	The Fermangh Story	Enniskillen 1969
Lydon, James (Ed.)	England and Ireland in the Later Middle Ages	Blackrock 1981
Mac Neill, Maire	The Festival of Lughnasa	Dublin 1982
Mac Niocaill, Gearoid	Na Manaigh Liatha in Eirinn 1142- ca. 1600	Blackrock 1959
Mac Niocaill	Ireland before the Vikings	Dublin 1972
Martin, F.X.	The Pre-Reformation Augustinian Friaries	Dublin 1956
Maxwell, Constancia	Irish History from Contemporary sources (1509 –1610)	London, 1923
McCone, K,& Simms, C.	Progress in Medieval Irish Studies	Maynooth 1996
McCormick, Anthony M	The Earldom of Desmond	Dublin 2005
Meehan. Rev. C.P.	The Rise and fall of the Franciscan Monasteries	Dublin 1877
McNeill, T E.	Anglo Norman Ulster	Edinburgh 1980
Moore, M.J. (Ed.)	Archaeological Inventory of Co. Wexford	Dublin 1996
Navanlinna, S, & Taavitsainan, I.	A Late M.E. Life of St. Katherine of Alexandria	Woodbridge 1993
O Conchur, Donocha,	Corca Dhuibhne,	Dublin 1973
O Corrain, Donnchadh (Ed.)	Peritia, Volume 14	Turnhout 2000
O hOgain, Daithi	The Sacred Isle	Cork 1999
O'Keefe, Tadhg	An Anglo Norman Monastery	Kinsale 1999

Orpen, G.H.	Ireland under the Normans 1169- 1333	Oxford 1968
Otway-Ruthven,. A.J.	A History of Medieval Ireland	London 1968
Papaioannou, Evangelos	The Monastery of St. Catherine	
Picard, Jean -Michel (Ed.)	Aquitaine and Ireland in the Middle Ages	Blackrock 1995
Power Rev Patrick	Placenames of the Decies (2nd Ed)	Cork 1952
Power, Rev Patrick	Waterford and Lismore : A compendious history	Cork 1937
Rackard, A and O' Callaghan L	Fishstonewater: Holy Wells of Ireland	Cork, 2001
Reeves, William	The Eccliesiastical History of the Dioceses of Down and Connor	Dublin 1847
Richter, Michael	Medieval Ireland, the Enduring Traditioin	Dublin 1988
Saul, Nigel	The Oxford Illustrated History of England	Oxford 1997
Sheehy, Maurice P.	Pontiflcia Hibemica (2 Vols.)	Dublin 1962, 1965
Silke, Rev. John	The Diocese of Raphoe: -a Brief History	Strasbourg 1997
Stokes, Whteley (Ed.)	Feffire Hui Ghormain	London 1985
Walsh, Rev. Paul	Leabhar Chloinne Suibhne (The Book of the MacSweeneys)	Dublin 1920
Watt, Morrell, and Martin.	Medieval Studies presented to Aubrey Gwynn	Dublin 1961

MAPS   PAGE

PLANS

ILLUSTRATIONS (Figures)

Pamphlets Consulted

1) Anonymous	A Guide to St Doulagh's Church	Doulagh's Heritage Project	Paceprint Dublin	N.D.
2) Anonymous	St Catherine's Parish Conna/Ballynoe/Glengoura	Litho Press	Middleton	(2000)
3) Crawford, John	St. Catherine's Parish Church, Dublin	Irish Academic Press	Blackrock	(1996)
4) Cunningham J.B.	Lough Derg, Legendary Pilgrimage	RES. Printers	Monaghan	(1984)
5) Egan Patrick K. CC	Clonfert Museum and Its Collections	Galway A.H.S.J	Galway	(1948)
6) Fenning, Hugh OP.	The Black Abbey (Kilkenny)	The Kilkenny People	Kilkenny	(1996)
7) Fraher, William	The Augustinians in Abbeyside (1290-1990)	The 700 Committee	Dungarvan	(1996)
8) French, Noel E.	Trim, Places and Traces	Meath Heritage Centre	Trim	N.D.
9) Froude, James Anthony	The Dissolution of the Monasteries	Frazers' Magazine	London	(1857)
10) Giff, Rev. W.C.M	St. Patrick's Cathedral, Trim	Longford Printing Co.	Longford	(1959)
11) Liston, Bríd FCJ	Sacred Places and Pilgrimages in Archdiocese of Dublin	Veritas	Dublin	(2000)
12) Loeber, Rolf	English Colonisation in Ireland (1534-1609)	Irish Historical Settlement	Athlone	(1991)
13) OCarragain, Eamonn	The City of Rome and Bede	Jarrow Lecture	Newcastle upon Tyne	(1994)
14) O'Donnell, Terence	OCM Franciscan Donegal	Franciscan Friary	Ros Nuala	(1952)
15) Papaioannow, Evangelos	The Monastery of St. Catherine	Japhet Press	Mt. Sinai	(1976)
16) Phelan, Tommy	Handbury Lane from Whence I came	U. Maynooth	Maynooth	(1998)
17) Roe, Helen M.	Medieval Fonts of Meath	Meath A.H.	Longford	(1968)
18) Seymour St. John D,	The Twelth Century Reformation in Ireland	APCK	Dublin	(1932)
19) Trench, C.E.F.	Slane	An Taisce, Meath	Kilrian	(1995)
20) Walsh, Paul Walsh	The Four Masters and their Work	At the Three Candles	Dublin	(1944)

INDEX   (Acknowledgments, Footnotes Omitted)

Conwal (nr.Letterkenny) (church site) 109

Coptic monks   27

Corcaguiny (Corca Dhuibne) (Co. Kerry) 70

Cork   15, 17, 21, 27, 30, 33, 45, 52-53, 58, 66-67, 74, 76, 81, 104-105, 107, 113

Cork and South Eastern Region 67

Cornmarket, Dublin   46, 47

Corporation Parks Department 65

Council Decrees   85-86

Council of Trent   107

Council of Anjou   34

Counties Somerset and Gloucestershire 34

Craobhscaoileadh Chlainne Suibhne, An   90, 91

Crawford's map   55

Croagh, The (see Croagh Patrick) 116

Croagh Patrick   86, 94

Crom Cruaic   116-118

Crom Dubh (see Crom Cruaic) 118

Cromwell(ian)   109

Crown, The   68

Crumlin (Co. Antrim)   77

Crutch Friars (Order)   81

Cumin, Archbishop of Dublin 46, 59

Curtis, Edmund   70

Dair Inis (see Molana)   76

Danes   46

Dearcu   27

de Bineford, John (cleric)   79

Decretal Letter (papal)   74

Dúchas   111

Decies, Lord of   101

Dedicatory altars   39

de Hereford, Adam   58, 59

de Kavesham, William   59

de Lacy Castle, Kells   36

Delle Vigne, Father   41

Denny, Sir Edward   121

de Pontfarcy, Yoland   106

Derry (diocese)   81

De Sandford, Fulk   59

Desart family   103

Desmond(s)   17, 101

Dickinson, Rev. J. C   46

Dingle (Co. Kerry)   45, 70, 71, 121

Dingleycuish (see Dingle)   70

Dissolution (see Henrician)   53, 55

Dominican(s) (Order) (Co. Meath) 40, 41, 76, 97

Donaghpatrick (Co. Meath) (church site) 83-84, 117, 118

Donegal (county)   16, 87, 107, 109-110, 119

Donore Avenue (Dublin)   55

Do-olaf (see St. Olaf)   62

Dowdall, Nicholas (cleric)   61

Down and Connor (diocese)   75, 77, 78

Downpatrick (Co. Down)   75, 77

Dromore (diocese)   77, 78

Drumcondra, Dublin   64, 65

Dublin   15, 17, 21, 27, 30, 33-34, 39, 45-48, 52-53, 57, 59, 62, 64, 72, 81, 86, 90, 105, 111

Duleek (Co. Meath)   50, 111

Dunbrody (Co. Wexford)   99, 101

Duncannon (Co. Wexford)   98, 101

Dungarvan (Co. Waterford)   53, 101, 109

Dunmoylan (Co. Limerick)   79

Dun na Mainistreach (Co. Waterford) (see Abbeyside) 109

Dunning, Rev. P.J   35, 53

du Noyer (George)   99

Dunsany (Co. Meath)   111

Earl(dom) of Desmond   67, 78, 109

Earl of Meath   55, 86

Early Christian Ireland   71

Early History of St. Thomas' Abbey, Dublin   46

Egan, Rev. Patrick   96

Elizabethan   18, 96

    -   Commission   97

Elizabethan Fiants   78

Elizabeth, Queen   79, 86, 97, 119